55 YEARS of EAST ANGLIAN STEAM

by Dr. Ian C. Allen

Oxford Publishing Co.

ISBN 086093 182 X

Typeset by Aquarius Typsetting Services, New Milton, Hants.

Published by
Oxford Publishing Co.
Link House
West Street
Poole, Dorset

65 YEARS of EAST ANGLIAN STEAM

OPC

Oxford Publishing Co.

SBN 86093 182 X

Foreword

To Bill Last, British Railways, Cambridge

Bill Last was born at Stonham Aspall, near Stowmarket in Suffolk. His father was a steam haulage contractor, so Bill grew up with steam and developed an interest in it from his earliest days — an interest which has never left him. In the 1920s, tractors were beginning to oust steam on the farms and Bill's father moved to Cambridge which, at this time, was a very flourishing railway centre. Before the grouping of the railways in 1923, Cambridge was served by the Great Eastern, Great Northern, London & North Western and Midland Railway Companies using one station with its unique platform for both up and down trains. On leaving school, Bill, with his knowledge of steam, was immediately accepted, in October 1932, by the LNER as a fitter apprentice at Cambridge. In July 1936, he was transferred to the footplate department and became a cleaner, in June 1937 a 'passed' cleaner (available for firing), in May 1942 a fireman, in May 1948 a 'passed' fireman (available for driving) and finally, in October 1954, a regular driver.

Just as tractors had ousted steam from the farms, so, by 1960, diesel locomotives were ousting steam from the railway followed later, in the 1970s, by electric trains coming to Royston from Kings Cross. But whilst learning the new techniques, Bill remained faithful to his first love, steam, and when Alan Bloom opened his live railway museum at Bressingham, near Diss in Norfolk, he became one of his principal drivers. No truer East Anglian lover of steam could ever have been found.

In 1924, the first Great Eastern locomotive I ever saw was *Claud Hamilton* in the early LNER livery. About this time, I started taking railway photographs and in this book, I have tried to show the world of steam in which Bill grew up and spent so much of his working life. After 49½ years of continuous working on the railway at Cambridge, Bill decided to take an early retirement in April 1982. With his knowledge and experience now gone, the railway at Cambridge will never quite be the same again.

With Bill being attached to Cambridge depot, his Ministry of Transport route card shows that in his heyday, he was passed for driving over 2,000 route miles.

The routes were:-

1) Cambridge to Liverpool St., including the loops round Stratford and Temple Mills to Thames Haven via Forest Gate Junction, Barking, Grays and Tilbury.

2) Cambridge to Kings Cross, including the Hertford loop and Finsbury Park to Broad St.

3) Cambridge to King's Lynn and Hunstanton, both via Ely and via the loop through St. Ives, March and Wisbech. Also St. Ives to Ely via Sutton.

4) Cambridge to Norwich and Yarmouth Vauxhall.

5) Cambridge to Colchester via (i) Newmarket, Bury St. Edmunds and Ipswich, (ii) via Sudbury and, (iii) via The Colne Valley line by way of Halstead. Also Colchester to Clacton and Bartlow to Audley End.

6) Cambridge to Mildenhall, and Newmarket to Ely via Fordham Junction.

7) Cambridge to Bedford, Bletchley and Oxford, (the former LNWR line).

8) Cambridge to St. Ives, Kimbolton and Kettering, (the former Midland line).

His duties have included firing on both the Royal engines, LNER 4-4-0s Nos. 8783 and 8787 when working the Royal Train between Kings Cross and King's Lynn for Sandringham, and driving Royalty when they have been travelling from Liverpool St. to King's Lynn in a special saloon attached to a normal service train.

He has also worked over many other East Anglian branch lines with the services of a pilotman.

My destiny led me to East Suffolk, therefore the line I know best is the one from Ipswich to Yarmouth and Lowestoft, one of the few lines Bill did not know. This line was built in 1859 very cheaply, with few earthworks and many level crossings. By the late-1950s the cost of maintenance of these crossing was becoming so high that in 1959 the Yarmouth traffic was routed via Norwich, giving a faster service. The direct line to Beccles was severed by the removal of the swing bridges, although relatively modern, at St. Olaves and Beccles. The East Suffolk line thus became a local branch from Ipswich to Lowestoft. As the natural traffic flow had always been to Yarmouth, receipts slumped and the line was soon a candidate for Dr. Beeching's axe. However, thanks to some determined opposition by the East Suffolk Travellers' Association, it became one of the very few lines to escape its prescribed fate, proving to be a social necessity. It is to be hoped that its future will be assured when electric trains come to Ipswich. In preparing this book I have been surprised at the thriving East Suffolk main line shown by my photographs twenty five years ago, so different from the rural branch line it has become today.

Ian C. Allen
March 1982

MAP 1: Routes worked by driver Last, in relation to East Anglia as a whole (not to scale).

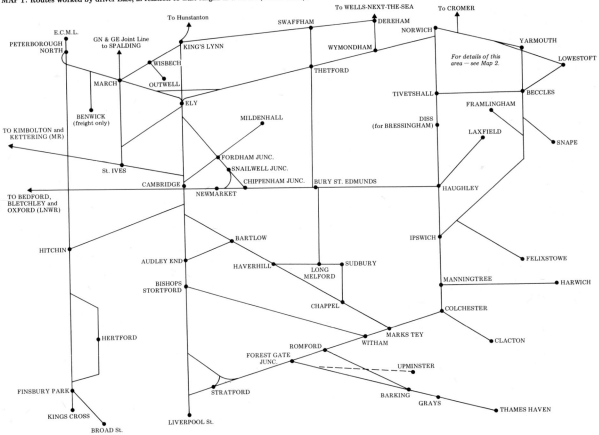

MAP 2: Lines in the Norwich, Cromer, Yarmouth and Lowestoft areas (not to scale).

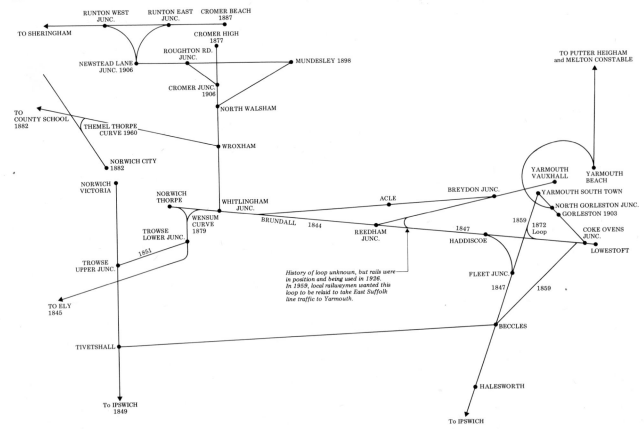

55 YEARS of EAST ANGLIAN STEAM

by Dr. Ian C. Allen

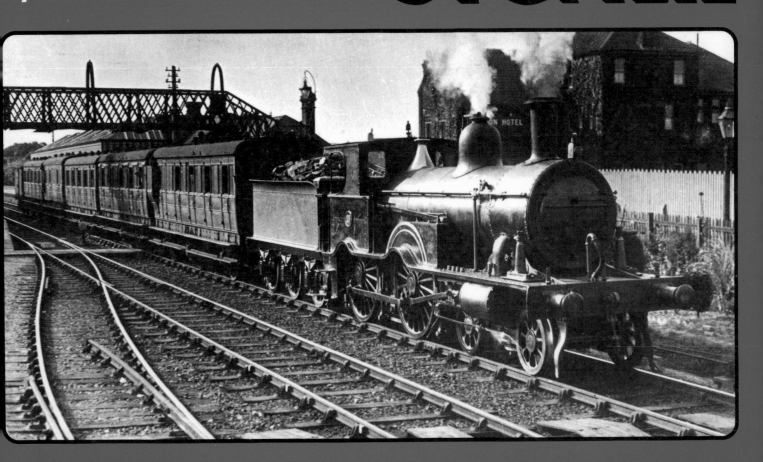

Chapter One — The Routes to East Anglia

Plate 1: Liverpool St., opened by the Great Eastern Railway in 1874, replacing the old terminus at Bishopsgate, has always been the normal gateway for travellers to East Anglia. This scene shows the afternoon Norwich and Cromer express about to leave Liverpool St. in July 1930. The locomotive is LNER Class B12, 4-6-0 No. 8523. This was one of three locomotives fitted experimentally, in 1927, with ACFI feed water heating apparatus. A further fifty Class B12, 4-6-0s were similarly fitted in the early-1930s. The very smoky atmosphere of the terminus is clearly shown.

MAP 3: M & GN system and GER lines in relation to this system (not to scale).

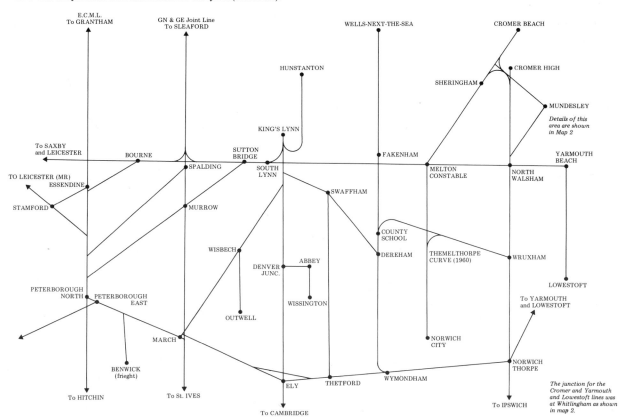

Plate 2: This view shows a Cambridge express about to leave Liverpool St. on the same afternoon in 1930 as in Plate 1. The locomotive is LNER Class D16/1, 4-4-0 No. 8805. This locomotive was, in 1923, the first 'Claud Hamilton' 4-4-0 to be rebuilt with a larger boiler fitted with top feed. It was soon known as a 'Super Claud', a name which stuck to the class all its life. It was not fitted with an extended smoke box until 1931. The top feed apparatus was subsequently removed, as was the brass beading on the cab sides, so that the number could be painted on more neatly. LNER 4-4-0s, Nos. 8783 and 8787, for years the Royal locomotives at Cambridge, were built in 1923 at Stratford.

Plate 3: Another scene photographed on the same day as the previous two, shows a Southend express about to depart behind Class B12, 4-6-0 No. 8574. This was one of ten locomotives built in 1928 by Beyer Peacock & Co. These had extended smoke boxes and were fitted with Lentz valve gear. This was removed from No. 8574 in 1932 and the locomotive was rebuilt to Class B12/3 with a larger boiler in 1933. These ten locomotives thus had a very short life in the original condition shown in this photograph.

Plate 4: The Great Northern Railway reached Cambridge, and thus East Anglia, by way of a branch from Hitchin. After the 1923 grouping, the Royal Train for King's Lynn and Wolferton began to take this route as did the 'Pullman Specials' for Newmarket races. This photograph shows LNER Class D2 4-4-0 No. 4326 on a Hitchin to Cambridge local train near Harston.

Plate 5: A scene showing Class A1, 4-6-2 No. 2561 *Minoru* on a down Newmarket 'race special' near Harston in 1931. The Pacifics were turned at Newmarket on the Snailwell Junction to Chippenham Junction triangle. They were a very tight fit through the Newmarket tunnel.

Plate 6: In the early-1930s, the Kings Cross to Cambridge service was largely worked by the Great Northern large boilered Class C1 Atlantics. This view shows one of this class, No. 4409. It is working an up Grimsby express and is recovering from a signal check near Peterborough. This photograph has been chosen for two reasons. Firstly, Peterborough may be regarded as one of the gateways to East Anglia from the Midlands and the North and, secondly, it shows three six-wheeled coaches in the make up of the train, as late as June 1932. To have descended Stoke Bank on an express in one of these vehicles is to have known the real sensation of speed on the railway.

Plate 7: The Midland & Great Northern Joint Railway was the only rival to the Great Eastern Railway in East Anglia. It ran from Yarmouth Beach and served North Norfolk. At Sutton Bridge it divided, with one line making an end-on Junction with a Midland Railway branch near Saxby, and another which ran via Wisbech North to Peterborough. It remained independent until taken over by the LNER in October 1936. In this scene, LNER 4-4-0 No. 076 is waiting at Peterborough North, in August 1938, to pick up the through Cromer coaches off a Kings Cross express. No. 076 was an ex-M&GN locomotive which had been built in 1899 to S. W. Johnson's standard design for the Midland Railway. It was taken into LNER stock and the prefix 'O' added to its original number, thus reviving a very old Stratford tradition.

Plate 8: The M&GN line through Bourne carried heavy traffic to and from East Anglia and the Midlands. Bourne was also the junction for a Great Northern branch to Essendine. Probably one of the more pleasant ways of slipping into East Anglia was by rail from Stamford. From here a GNR branch ran to Essendine, on the East Coast Main Line, where one crossed the footbridge and joined another GNR branch train which ran to Bourne, through Braceboro Spa. In September 1928, the restaurant car on the M&GN express train from Leicester to Yarmouth Beach was a twelve-wheeled Midland Railway car still lettered Midland and Glasgow & South Western Railway. The cutlery and antimacassars were also marked. The car had been used on the St. Pancras to St. Enoch (Glasgow) through expresses. Five of these cars were built in 1914, three were lettered Midland and Glasgow & South Western Railway and two, Midland Railway. It is one of the two Midland cars which is now preserved in the National Railway Museum at York. To have had tea in this car whilst climbing up through Thursford at 17 m.p.h. is to have known the golden age of railways. This picture shows an ex-M&GN 4-4-0 No. 025 at Bourne. The line to Saxby is on the right and that to Essendine, on the left. No. 025 was originally built in 1883 by Beyer Peacock for the Lynn & Fakenham Railway, becoming No. 25 in that company's list.

Plate 9: East Anglia could also be entered from the north via the GN&GE joint line from Doncaster through Lincoln, Spalding and March. Its value to the GER was that it gave access to the coalfields. It is hard, today, to imagine the endless stream of coal trains which used this line, loaded on the up, and empty on the down. This photograph shows LNER Class D3, 4-4-0 No. 4341 on an up van train near Helpringham. All except the first six vans are freshly painted 'GE' although the picture was taken in 1928. Cambridge locomotive sheds requirements were two long coal trains daily.

Plate 10: Providing he had plenty of time, the connoisseur of rail travel to East Anglia always tried to travel from Euston. Firstly, the Great Hall had to be visited to appreciate its glorious architecture. For 130 years this magnificent building put travellers from Euston into a state of pleasurable excitement about their journey. It survived Hitler's air bombardment, but fell victim to British Rail's demolition when they built their new terminus at Euston. Fortunately, the statue of George Stephenson, which dominated the Hall, has now been preserved and now presides benignly over the National Railway Museum at York. Then followed a visit to the booking office where the clerks were always helpful and polite. They were delighted to book you either to Swansea via Shrewsbury, to Cambridge via Bletchley, or to Peterborough via Rugby or Northampton. The fares were all competitive with the direct routes on which you could return, by means of a reciprocal agreement, with the same ticket if you were in a hurry. This picture shows the recently reboilered 4 cylinder 'Claughton' Class 4-6-0 No. 5948 *Baltic* at Bletchley in April 1932. No. 5948 had also been fitted with Caprotti valve gear. It had come off its train to pick up a horse box, which can be seen behind the tender. This had just arrived from Cambridge behind the 'Experiment' Class 4-6-0 seen on the left. The box contained, so an inspector told me, a very important horse from Newmarket. Rugby was ultimately reached twenty minutes late, but as I was travelling to Sheringham, stopping at every station en route, twenty minutes was neither here nor there.

Plate 11: This photograph shows LMS 'Experiment' Class 4-6-0 No. 5454 *Sarmatian* leaving Cambridge in 1932 on a freight train for Bedford and Bletchley. This locomotive makes an interesting comparison with the GER Class B12, 4-6-0s shown in Plates 1 and 3. The first Class B12 was built at Stratford in 1911 and the first 'Experiment' at Crewe in 1905. When Bill Last first joined the LNER at Cambridge, he never would have thought that one day he would be driving 'Claud Hamilton' 4-4-0s to Oxford over this route.

Plate 12: This view shows LMS 'Precursor' Class 4-4-0 No. 5271 *Gaelic* leaving Cambridge, also in 1932. *Gaelic* makes an interesting comparison with LNER 'Claud Hamilton' Class 4-4-0 No. 8866 shown in Plate 17. The first 'Precursor' was built at Crewe in 1904 and the first 'Claud Hamilton' at Stratford in 1900. In the early-1930s, the LMS was still running a 'start of term special' from Bletchley to Cambridge, only calling at Bedford, with five LNWR six-wheelers hauled by an 'Experiment' Class 4-6-0. This was an exhilarating way of entering East Anglia.

Plate 13: If, however, one went to St. Pancras and asked the booking clerk for a ticket to Cambridge via Kettering, or Bristol via Derby, one received a very rude reception. This was a pity, as Midland Railway restaurant car breakfasts were amongst the best in the country. The Midland line from Kettering to Cambridge was lightly laid with many weak bridges, and was worked by 2-4-0s, with small MR 0-6-0s on the freight trains. An old outside framed Kirtley 2-4-0, No. 12, later LMS No. 20012, used to work to Cambridge regularly through the 1930s and early-1940s. It is incredible that Bill Last should have fired No. 20012 which was built in 1867. Matthew Kirtley was appointed CME to the Midland Railway in 1844, having been born in 1813. According to history, he drove the first train from Birmingham to Euston, and incidentally hit the buffer stops. This photograph shows sister locomotive No. 21, built in 1868, on a Peterborough train near Helpston in 1932. Before nationalization in 1948, there was an LMS link at Cambridge composed of two regular drivers and two regular 'passed' firemen, the latter being able to take over a driver's duty if necessary. When this occurred, a LNER 'passed' cleaner or fireman would take over the LMS fireman's duty. This was how Bill Last came to fire on LMS locomotives.

Plate 14: A photograph showing Johnson LMS 2-4-0 No. 240 approaching Chesterton Junction on a Cambridge to Kettering train in 1931. Bill Last also fired locomotives of this type on the LMS line to Kettering.

Chapter Two — Some East Anglian Trains in the 1930s

In this chapter I have tried to show pictorially what the trains were like when Bill Last joined the LNER at Cambridge, in the 1930s.

Plate 15: This shows LNER Class E4, 2-4-0 No. 2785 on a heavy Bury St. Edmunds to Ipswich train. This locomotive, which is now preserved in the National Railway Museum at York, was built at Stratford in 1895 to Holden's 1891 design. It was the last 2-4-0 still working in this country when it was withdrawn in 1959. Bill Last knew these locomotives well at Cambridge. They were extensively used all over East Anglia being able to cope with nearly every type of traffic with the exception of expresses and heavy coal trains. This picture was actually taken in August 1949. The class was never altered externally except for the replacement of their GER stovepipe chimneys in the early-1930s by one of the more graceful LNER designs. It is still recalled in railway circles at Cambridge how, in the last year or two of the Great Eastern Railway, the then Prince of Wales suddenly asked for a special train to take him and his lady friend urgently from a Newmarket race meeting to London. A three coach special was hastily provided, hauled by the only available locomotive, a Class E4, 2-4-0. In spite of its 5 ft. 7 in. driving wheels, it ran up from Cambridge, a distance of 55¾ miles, in under an hour.

Plate 16: This photograph shows L N E R Class D13, 4-4-0 No. 7700 entering Newmarket on a Cambridge to Ipswich train in 1931. The Class D13 locomotives had originally been designed in 1886 as a standard 2-4-0 express passenger type, to replace an assortment of older locomotives. When they in turn were replaced on the expresses by the 'Claud Hamilton' 4-4-0s, most were superheated and fitted with a bogie off withdrawn 0-4-4 tank engines, thus becoming 4-4-0s, like No. 7700. The last of this class survived at Cambridge until 1944 and is well remembered by Bill Last.

Plate 17: *Claud Hamilton*, the first of the famous G E Class of 4-4-0, was built at Stratford in 1900. By the 1930s, the class had been modernised with superheated boilers and extended smoke boxes. This view shows L N E R Class D15/2, 4-4-0 No. 8866 working an Ely to Cambridge local near Chesterton Junction in 1931 in its modernised state. Bill Last tells me that in order to get the best out of these locomotives, there had to be a perfect understanding between driver and fireman. They were not particularly free steamers and too heavy a driver could, more or less, murder his fireman who would have to shift many more hundredweights of coal than he would for a lighter driver. However, too light a driver would not create a sufficient draught to produce a full head of steam. It is curious how the skills of a fireman have never been fully appreciated, considering that ultimately the proper functioning of the whole railway system depended on him. If he could not provide enough steam for his driver, the latter, however able, could not keep his train to time and delays would consequently snowball all over the area. Traditionally, before the 1939—45 war, a fireman could not expect to be a driver for a least twenty years. It takes about six years to become a doctor. It is interesting to compare this photograph with Plate 12 which shows the L N W R 'Precursor' Class 4-4-0 locomotive.

Plate 18: LNER Class D15/2, 'Claud Hamilton' 4-4-0 No. 8871 photographed near Manningtree in 1938 on an up local train. To assist steaming, the original Stratford chimney was replaced, in the mid-1930s, on all members of the class by one of Doncaster pattern as shown here.

Plate 19: Plate 2 showed LNER Class D16/1, 4-4-0 No. 8805, the first 'Claud Hamilton' to be rebuilt with a larger boiler. Subsequently another thirty nine were similarly rebuilt though they were soon fitted with extended smoke boxes and had the top feed removed. This picture shows LNER 'Super Claud' 4-4-0, Class D16/2 No. 8851 running with this later modification. This view was taken in 1936 near Brandon and shows the Liverpool to Lowestoft through restaurant car express. The train is composed of eleven GCR-type bogies. It is interesting that the 'Super Claud' 4-4-0s always retained their Stratford chimneys.

Plate 20: After forty 'Clauds' had been rebuilt as 'Super Clauds' with Belpaire fire boxes, all subsequent rebuilds were to Class D16/3 with round topped fire boxes. This picture shows such a rebuild, BR Class D16/3, 4-4-0 No. 62615. It is seen working the heaviest train of the day on the East Suffolk line as late as August 1949. This train ran from Liverpool St. to Yarmouth South Town, its first stop being Manningtree. It is shown passing Wickham Market Junction. At this time, large numbers of standard Class B1 4-6-0s were being built, and very soon they replaced the 'Clauds' on all the hardest duties.

Plate 21: This scene shows one of the Holden Class B12, 4-6-0s No. 8520 climbing up to Dullingham with a heavy Newmarket to Liverpool St. race special. The Pullman and 1st class specials ran to Kings Cross. These locomotives were introduced in 1911 to replace the 'Claud Hamilton' 4-4-0s on the heaviest duties. They had long capacious cabs and were not much larger than the 4-4-0s being built at the same time by other railway companies. Ultimately, eighty were built; the last in 1928 *(see Plate 3)*. Their boilers were standard with those fitted to the Class J20 0-6-0s.

Plate 22: In the 1930s and 1940s, most of the Holden Class B12, 4-6-0s were rebuilt with larger boilers, becoming Class B12/3. This photograph shows Class B12/3 No. 8510 at Ipswich in August 1939 on a down summer Saturday Yarmouth express. The stock is an experimental set built at Stratford in 1900 which spent all its life on suburban duties. The passenger peering between the bars must have had quite an interesting journey. The use of old non-lavatory suburban stock for lengthy weekend journeys was typical of the period and one which required a very co-operative guard.

◁ *Plate 23 (top left):* Many of the locomotive problems on the Great Eastern section were solved by the introduction, in 1928, of Gresley's 3 cylinder 'Sandringham' Class B17, 4-6-0s, though there were many teething troubles. In this picture, taken near Claydon in 1936, LNER 3 cylinder Class B17, 4-6-0 No. 2807 *Blickling*, is shown working a Norwich to Ipswich local train. At this time, No. 2807's usual duty was to work the 'North Country Continental Express', which gave a through service from Parkston Quay to Liverpool and York, from Ipswich to Manchester, returning next day, alternating with a Gorton-based 'Sandringham' Class locomotive. On the third day, after acting as standby locomotive for the express, it worked a local to Norwich and back, as shown in this photograph.

◁ *Plate 24 (middle left):* This view shows LNER Class F3, 2-4-2T No. 8043 approaching Thorpeness Halt on the Aldeburgh branch in 1938. The very lightly laid track will be noted, with re-sleepering in progress.

◁ *Plate 25 (bottom left):* In the late-1920s, the LNER bought from the government a large number of Robinson Class 04, 2-8-0s that had originally been built for use in the 1914—18 war. This resulted in a surplus of locomotives on the GC section, and several of these found their way into East Anglia. This picture shows a former GC locomotive, LNER Class C14, 4-4-2T No. 6120 leaving Westerfield Junction on a Felixstowe to Ipswich train. The Felixstowe branch was always difficult to work owing to a great seasonal fluctuation in passenger traffic. I can remember seeing, on Whit Sunday 1938, a Cambridge to Felixstowe (via the Colne Valley line) excursion, which comprised eleven 'Flying Scotsman' coaches, complete with headboards. It was hauled by two 'covered wagon' Class J15 0-6-0s. This was the name given, at Cambridge, to the five J15s fitted with tender cabs for tender-first working over the Colne Valley branch.

Plate 26: During the 1930s, the Midland & Great Northern Joint line conveyed very heavy passenger traffic on Saturdays from the Midlands through to Yarmouth. There was also a flourising seasonal agricultural and fish traffic with 'fisher girls' coming down annually from north-east Scotland to cope with the herring season. The M&GN locomotives were Victorian, mostly of S. W. Johnson's standard Derby design, and were painted a golden yellow. The works was situated at Melton Constable where its chief engineer from 1884 to 1924 was Mr William Marriott. His chief draughtsman was Mr G. B. Clark. In 1958, Mr Clark told me how he had arrived at Melton Constable on a snowy January day in 1892, being hauled from South Lynn by one of the Cornish Mineral Railway 0-6-0 tanks which had just been rebuilt as a 2-4-0 tender locomotive. In his hall, there was a large diagram of a small London Tilbury & Southend 4-4-2T which he had drawn as an apprentice. He was, however, reticent about how much he had been responsible for the design of the three M&GN 4-4-2 tanks and how many old parts were used in these rebuilds. Melton Constable was not allowed to build new locomotives, only repair them. He was also reticent about the M&GN 0-6-0 tanks, nominally rebuilds of the old Cornish Mineral Railway 0-6-0 tanks. He said that Mr Marriott was Derby's blue-eyed boy and that he used to go there every month, and was given whatever he asked for. In showing me over the remains of the works, he made the whole of the previous sixty years come vividly alive. He also showed me, with great pride, what the company had done for the welfare of the men of the town. The works closed in 1936 and the maintenance of the locomotives was transferred to Stratford, except for the twelve Class J3, 0-6-0s which were sent to Doncaster. Bill Last knew the M&GN locomotives when they passed through Cambridge on their way to or from Stratford for repair or scrap. This scene shows a typical M&GN local train near Mundesley, in North Norfolk, in 1928. It is hauled by M&GN 0-6-0 No. 63 and is working a Cromer Beach to Yarmouth Beach service. It is interesting to note that Samuel Johnson was CME at Stratford from 1866 to 1873. The family likeness between M&GN 0-6-0 No. 63 and the 0-6-0s he built for the GER in 1867 is very pronounced. Samuel Johnson was appointed CME of the NBR at Cowlairs in 1864 at the age of thirty three.

Plate 27 (top left): Four of the small 0-6-0s were rebuilt with larger boilers, similar to the Class 3 Midland Railway 0-6-0s. This view shows M&GN rebuilt 0-6-0 No. 62 on a freight train near Massingham in August 1936.

Plate 28 (bottom left): The principal M&GN passenger locomotives were 4-4-0s, similar to those being built by Derby in the 1890s for the Midland Railway. There originally were forty of this class on the M&GN of which ten were subsequently rebuilt with larger boilers. This photograph shows an unrebuilt M&GN 4-4-0 No. 78 piloting a rebuilt 4-4-0 No. 39 on a train of GNR six wheel coaches. The train was climbing up from Melton Constable in September 1928.

Plate 29: In the early-1930s, a few of the unrebuilt M&GN 4-4-0s were fitted with small Belpaire boilers, similar to those being fitted, at Derby, to some of the Midland 2-4-0s and small 0-6-0s. This picture shows M&GN 4-4-0 No. 02 fitted with such a boiler. The photograph was taken near Caister-on-Sea in August 1938.

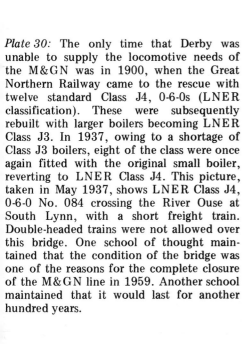

Plate 30: The only time that Derby was unable to supply the locomotive needs of the M&GN was in 1900, when the Great Northern Railway came to the rescue with twelve standard Class J4, 0-6-0s (LNER classification). These were subsequently rebuilt with larger boilers becoming LNER Class J3. In 1937, owing to a shortage of Class J3 boilers, eight of the class were once again fitted with the original small boiler, reverting to LNER Class J4. This picture, taken in May 1937, shows LNER Class J4, 0-6-0 No. 084 crossing the River Ouse at South Lynn, with a short freight train. Double-headed trains were not allowed over this bridge. One school of thought maintained that the condition of the bridge was one of the reasons for the complete closure of the M&GN line in 1959. Another school maintained that it would last for another hundred years.

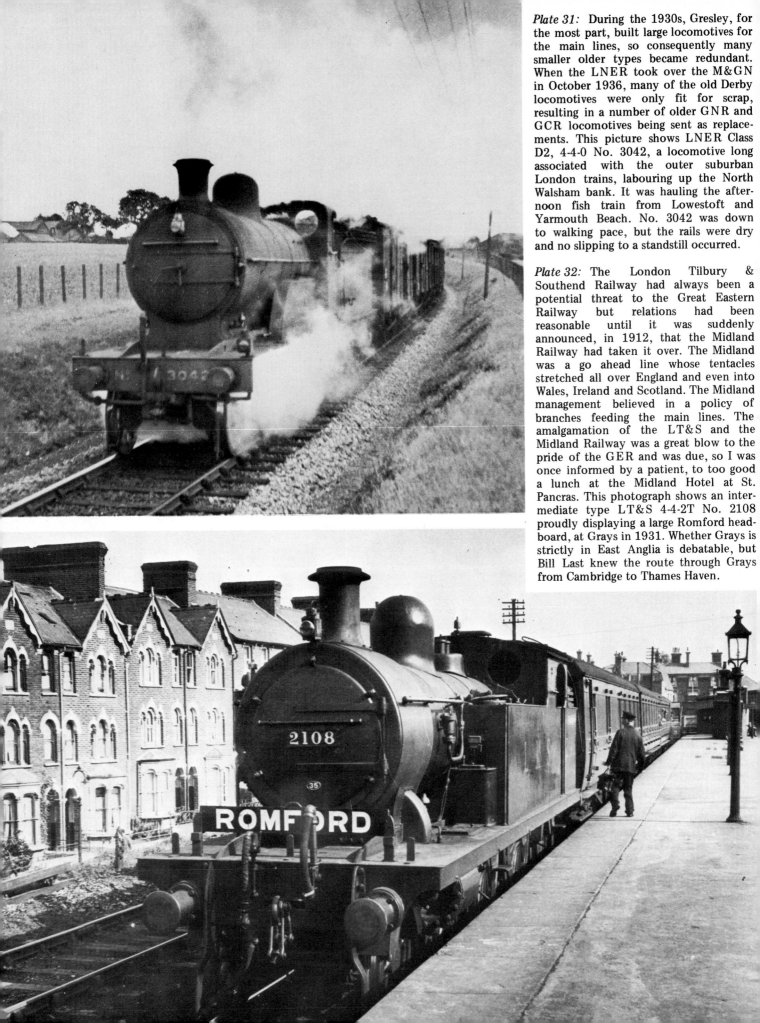

Plate 31: During the 1930s, Gresley, for the most part, built large locomotives for the main lines, so consequently many smaller older types became redundant. When the LNER took over the M&GN in October 1936, many of the old Derby locomotives were only fit for scrap, resulting in a number of older GNR and GCR locomotives being sent as replacements. This picture shows LNER Class D2, 4-4-0 No. 3042, a locomotive long associated with the outer suburban London trains, labouring up the North Walsham bank. It was hauling the afternoon fish train from Lowestoft and Yarmouth Beach. No. 3042 was down to walking pace, but the rails were dry and no slipping to a standstill occurred.

Plate 32: The London Tilbury & Southend Railway had always been a potential threat to the Great Eastern Railway but relations had been reasonable until it was suddenly announced, in 1912, that the Midland Railway had taken it over. The Midland was a go ahead line whose tentacles stretched all over England and even into Wales, Ireland and Scotland. The Midland management believed in a policy of branches feeding the main lines. The amalgamation of the LT&S and the Midland Railway was a great blow to the pride of the GER and was due, so I was once informed by a patient, to too good a lunch at the Midland Hotel at St. Pancras. This photograph shows an intermediate type LT&S 4-4-2T No. 2108 proudly displaying a large Romford headboard, at Grays in 1931. Whether Grays is strictly in East Anglia is debatable, but Bill Last knew the route through Grays from Cambridge to Thames Haven.

Plate 33: The 3 ft. gauge line from Halesworth to Southwold was opened in 1879 but was never a threat to the Great Eastern. This picture was taken in 1926 and shows 2-4-0T No. 3 *Blyth* entering Southwold. No. 3 was built by Sharp Stewart & Co. Ltd. in 1879. I can still remember my bitter disappointment at a journey in one of the tramway-type coaches. Passengers had to sit with their backs to the window, gazing at the passenger sitting opposite and owing to the narrow gauge, there was very little room for one's knees. Sometimes, in the autumn when the rails were greasy, the train would stall on the gradient up to Halesworth station. When this happened the two GER horses used for shunting the transfer traffic were summoned and the train would ultimately arrive with the two horses piloting the locomotive.

Plate 34: The Mid-Suffolk Light Railway was an independent line, opened for passenger traffic in 1908 from Haughley Junction, near Stowmarket, to the village of Laxfield. It had been hoped to reach Halesworth but, not surprisingly, funds ran out and the line finally petered out in the village of Cratfield. For a few years a freight train ran, as required, from Laxfield to Cratfield, until one day a farmer, going to collect a hen house, removed the station by mistake. The LNER wished to have nothing to do with the line at the 1923 grouping of railways. The story is still told how the local M.P. gave the Parliamentary Committee considering the matter a very good lunch. The LNER had to take the line over in June 1924. A patient I still sometimes see remembers, as a boy, being on the platform at Laxfield for the departure of the first train in 1908. Soon after this, his father moved his complete farm from Wisbech to Cratfield by rail. He tells me that the older people regarded a trip on the railway as a sure way of getting scarlet fever. He remembers what a good headmaster there was at Laxfield school, who unfortunately got the sack for devoting too much time to the promotion of the railway and not enough time to school affairs. It is difficult today to realize how very isolated country communities felt when horses were the only means of transport. This picture, taken in 1938, shows LNER Class J65, 0-6-0T No. 7155 approaching Laxfield. The staggering of the original sleepers, in order to find a sound piece of wood into which the spikes holding the flat-bottomed rails could be driven, will be noticed.

Chapter Three — The War Years and Final Decade of Steam

When the German invasion threatened England in 1940, East Anglia became an armed camp with thousands of troops under training. Later came the United States Air Force for the bombing of Germany.

There was a tremendous increase in railway traffic even on the remotest branch lines. Any undue interest in the railways could be interpreted as spying, and photography was impossible.

Thanks to people like Bill Last and all his railway colleagues, essential transport never failed, whatever the danger. Driver Benjamin Gimbert and Fireman James Nightall saved the village of Soham by their courage, the latter losing his life. They were both decorated with the George Cross and now, very belatedly, each has had a Class 47 diesel locomotive named after him. The signalman at Soham was also killed in the same bomb explosion.

Difficult conditions persisted long after hostilities ceased and it was not until the railway system was taken over by British Railways in 1948, that it was possible to record, once again, the railway scene.

In this chapter I have tried to show, pictorially, what railway travel was like in East Anglia during the 1950s. I should like the reader to imagine that he is arriving at Liverpool St. with a ticket giving him (say) a month's unlimited travel. He should take a train for Marks Tey where he should change on to the Cambridge train. He could then either get out at the first station, Chappel, and take the Colne Valley line to Haverhill, or continue in the Cambridge train to Long Melford. If he did the latter, he could go to Bury St. Edmunds and back before going on to Cambridge. If he changed at Chappel, he would arrive at Haverhill before the Cambridge train which went round via Sudbury. He could then rejoin it and continue his journey. At Bartlow, he could take the train to Audley End or he could go straight on to Cambridge, visiting Audley End on his way back to Marks Tey, where he could then take the train for Clacton, etc. I hope this paragraph, with the aid of the maps, will make it clear how I have arranged the photographs in this section.

Plate 35 (above): This photograph is Bill Last's favourite. It was taken in August 1960 at Liverpool St. and makes an interesting comparison with Plate 1 taken in 1930. The picture shows the same smoky atmosphere of the terminus. In the foreground is Class K3, 3 cylinder 2-6-0 No. 61942 about to depart on the early evening commuters' train to Harwich. A Class L1, 2-6-4T is leaving on a down Cambridge line slow, while 'Britannia' Class 4-6-2 No. 70035 *Rudyard Kipling* is about to depart on a Norwich express.

Plate 36 (above): In this view, Class B17/6, 3 cylinder 4-6-0 No. 61600 *Sandringham* is leaving Liverpool St. on a down slow in July 1957. *Sandringham* was withdrawn shortly afterwards.

Plate 37 (below): Marks Tey is the station before Colchester, and is the junction for the branch to Cambridge. This photograph shows Class D16/3, 4-4-0 No. 62532 entering Marks Tey on a Cambridge to Colchester train in October 1956. No. 62532 was withdrawn a few weeks later. One did not realize, at the time, how many locomotives were being withdrawn and how quickly the railway scene was changing. No. 62532 was one of ten 'Claud Hamilton' Class D16/3, 4-4-0s to be rebuilt with 9½in. piston valves making them very fine locomotives, though when working hard, Bill Last tells me, a certain 'give' in the frames could be felt.

Plate 38: This scene shows one of the large Class J20, 0-6-0s No. 64683 on a Cambridge to Colchester train near Marks Tey. This class was rare on passenger trains, being built to haul heavy coal trains up from Whitemoor to London via Cambridge. Most were not fitted with steam heating apparatus.

Plate 39: One of the most striking pieces of railway architecture in East Anglia is the Chappel viaduct, opened in 1849. This picture shows an ex-Southern Railway 5 ft. 7 in. 4-6-0 No. 841, now named *Greene King*, going one Sunday morning to Chappel. It was returning after one of its unlucky trips on the main line.

Plate 40: This photograph shows Class J15, 0-6-0 No. 65477 on a Cambridge to Colchester train leaving Chappel, crossing the viaduct.

Plate 41: In this view an Austerity 2-8-0 No. 90601 is seen on a Whitemoor to Marks Tey freight train near Long Melford in the mid-1950s. This route was used during the 1939—45 war to relieve congestion on the main Cambridge to London line, the signal boxes being manned all night.

Plate 42: A Class D16/3, 4-4-0 No. 62558 leaves Long Melford on a Cambridge to Colchester train. This locomotive had been rebuilt, in 1926, as a 'Super Claud'. and the hole in the splasher, where the top feed pipe went through, will be noted. No. 62558 was rebuilt again, in 1948, as a Class D16/3, being fitted with a boiler having a round-topped fire box. The Class B12/3, 4-6-0s, made redundant after the Southend electrification on 30th December 1956, were sent to Cambridge where, amongst other duties, they replaced the 'Claud Hamilton' 4-4-0s on the Colchester branch owing to their better weight distribution. Many bridges in East Anglia were becoming life expired, a factor which must have influenced the branch line closures effected a few years later.

Plate 43: This picture shows a former GNR locomotive, Class C12, BR 4-4-2T No. 67367 on a Long Melford to Bury St. Edmunds train near Long Melford.

Plate 46 (above): In this scene, an 0-6-0 Class J15, No. 65475, is seen on a Cambridge to Colchester train near Long Melford. It is approaching a level crossing which was kept by a Russian Princess. The coach next to the locomotive is the medical inspection saloon used for routine health and eyesight examinations at the various locomotive depots.

Plate 44 (left above): A vacuum fitted Class J17, 0-6-0 No. 65562 approaches Lavenham on a Bury St. Edmunds to Long Melford train, with an articulated two coach set. The vacuum brake had been fitted to No. 65562 during the 1939—45 war for working over the M&GN system. During the 1930s, both the GWR and the LMS had put in hand an extensive programme of replacing the older types of locomotives by modern standard designs. The LNER, particularly in the north-east, was badly hit by the depression, so Gresley tended to build modern locomotives for the main line, leaving the older locomotives to carry on working the branches. As a result East Anglia, in the 1950s, was full of a delightful assortment of elderly locomotives and one never knew what class would appear at the head of a train. Because of this, East Anglia was the first region to be fully dieselized and the first in which the new disease of 'steam starvation' made its appearance, a disease which is still endemic in the region.

Plate 45 (left below): An 0-6-0 Class J15, No. 65461, leaves Welnetham on a Bury St. Edmunds to Long Melford train. The station name board was of the original GER pattern and is now preserved in the National Railway Museum at York.

Plate 47: Class E4, 2-4-0 No. 62790 nears Glemsford on a Cambridge to Colchester train. The old GER distant signal, with its arm making a very sharp angle with the post, can be seen behind the steam. This signal was one of the last survivors of what had been normal Great Eastern practice.

Plate 48: The Colne Valley & Halstead Railway was a small East Anglian company which remained independent until the 1923 grouping. It was apparently rather resented by its powerful neighbour, the GER. The railway ran from Haverhill, through Halstead, to Chappel. The branch train via Halstead would leave Haverhill after the Sudbury line train had left, and yet reach Chappel before it, (and vice versa in the other direction). Because of this, the summer Cambridge to Clacton through train took almost the same time in 1958 to Colchester as it had in 1877. This photograph shows Ivatt Class 2-6-0 No. 46468 on a Colne Valley line train diverging from the Sudbury line near Haverhill.

Plate 49: This scene shows Class N7/3, 0-6-2T No. 69651 on the Haverhill to Audley End push and pull service which reversed at Bartlow, near Saffron Walden. Local opinion still believes that if Dr. Beeching had not closed this line, Haverhill might have succeeded as a London overspill town.

Plate 50: Class E4, 2-4-0 No. 62787 is pictured on a Cambridge to Colchester train near Pampisford.

Plate 51: This scene shows Class E4, 2-4-0 No. 62788, passing Cambridge South signal box, entering Cambridge on the Whittlesford freight train. At the time of writing the signal box was soon to be pulled down. The picture was taken in August 1957 and No. 62788 was withdrawn in March 1958. She had been put into store at Norwich in 1955 on the arrival of the first diesel railcars, and it was not thought that she would be steamed again. However, in March 1956, she was sent to Cambridge to work the Colchester branch, usually being out-shedded at Sudbury. In August 1957 she was relegated to the Whittlesford freight, her place at Sudbury being taken by sister locomotive No. 62783, a locomotive which, since 1954, had been shedded at Hitchin for working the weekend Henlow Camp train resulting in a weekly run of about 50 miles.

Plate 52: Returning from Cambridge to Marks Tey, the next station down the line is Colchester. This photograph shows an unusual visit of Class B2, 2 cylinder rebuilt 'Sandringham' 4-6-0 No. 61616 *Fallodon* to Colchester in August 1959 on a up Clacton express. This locomotive was withdrawn a month later. Soon after rebuilding, in 1945, No. 61616 had been sent to Colchester for working, together with other Class B2s, the Clacton interval expresses. Since 1956, it had been at Cambridge with nine other members of the class. The shed at Colchester always remained very primitive with rows of locomotives in the sidings outside. I once had the privilege of being shown over it. A test match was in progress at the time and two blasts on the whistle of the pilot locomotive meant that another Australian wicket had fallen. The shed master was a great cricketer. Bill Last spent some of his time as fireman on the spare Royal engine, Class B2 rebuilt 2 cylinder 'Sandringham' No. 61617 *Ford Castle*. Personally, he did not like it, finding it heavy on coal and water and requiring more lever to get it along than the unrebuilt 3 cylinder Class B17s of which he had a very good opinion.

Plate 53: Class B17/6, 3 cylinder 4-6-0 No. 61666 *Nottingham Forest* enters Wivenhoe on a down Clacton interval service express.

Plate 54: A small Ivatt 2-6-0 No. 46468 passes Parsons Heath on a Colchester to Harwich local train.

Plate 55: In this view 'Britannia' Class 4-6-2 No. 70034 *Thomas Hardy* is seen on an up express at Parsons Heath. There had been a landslide between there and Colchester and single line working was in operation. The driver has just received the order to proceed from the pilotman who is making his way back to the signal box.

Plate 56 (left above): The GER developed Parkeston Quay as a port for the continental traffic which was always regarded as a matter of great importance. This picture shows Class B1, 4-6-0 No. 61109 on the down 'Day Continental' at Manningtree, taking the junction points at 10 m.p.h. This junction has recently been completely remodelled.

Plate 57 (left below): Class N7/3, 0-6-2T No. 69731 approaches Mistley on a Harwich to Colchester local train. In the foreground, where the man is scything, the track bed of the original line to Mistley Quay can be seen. This was abandoned in the early 1890s when the present steep incline on the down side was built.

Plate 58: The GER Holden 0-6-0 tanks were very distinctive and ubiquitous. This photograph shows Class J69/1, 0-6-0T No. 68635 at Parkeston Quay in December 1961. No. 68635 had spent over 20 years in Scotland and was thus in its original condition with a low cab roof and a very dilapidated three piece stovepipe chimney. No. 68635 survived at Stratford until the end of steam in September 1962 but with a new rolled steel stovepipe chimney.

Plate 59: A Class B17/6, No. 61658 *The Essex Regiment* passes Bentley on the Edinburgh to Colchester through train. This train had been put on during the 1939—45 war when it was always packed. It survived into the diesel era, but latterly was little more than a parcels train. The Hadleigh branch freight train is seen in the background.

Plate 60: A scene showing Class B17/6, 3 cylinder 4-6-0 No. 61646 *Gilwell Park* working a Colchester to Ipswich local train near Bentley. The first forty eight 'Sandringhams', when they were built, had small tenders owing to the weight and length limitations on the Great Easter section. At times, the limited water and coal capacity of these small tenders could cause delay when a quick turn-round was required. Therefore, when it was necessary to increase the coal capacity, a stout wooden plank was fixed with fishplates, to the tender on the right hand side, and the left side was made up with large lumps of coal. By this means the coal capacity was increased by more than two tons. The wooden plank can be seen in this picture. No. 61666 normally worked on the Clacton internal service.

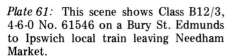

Plate 61: This scene shows Class B12/3, 4-6-0 No. 61546 on a Bury St. Edmunds to Ipswich local train leaving Needham Market.

Plate 62: The 'Britannias' were introduced into East Anglia in 1951 on the London to Norwich expresses. They were a much more powerful locomotive than had ever been used before on the GE section, with the exception of the experimental use, in 1949, of a Bulleid Southern Region Pacific, plus three more in regular use in 1950, and great accelerations were made in the timetables. This picture shows 'Britannia' Class 4-6-2 No. 70010 *Owen Glendower* on a down express at Haughley. The 'Britannias', in East Anglia, will always be associated with the name of Bill Harvey, the Norwich shed master, and probably one of the greatest steam locomotive engineers living today. No 70010 *Own Glendower* was his favourite 'Britannia'.

Plate 63: In 1933 the 'Claud Hamilton' 4-4-0s started to be rebuilt with large boilers having round topped fire boxes. During the next few years, in the course of rebuilding, ten were fitted with 8in. piston valves and ten with 9½in. valves. The latter proved to be brilliant performers, but, as was so common with rebuilds, they suffered from frame trouble. The piston valve locomotives could be recognised by their front end framing. This picture shows a 9½in. piston valve Class D16/3 'Claud Hamilton' 4-4-0 No. 62576 approaching Haughley on an Ipswich to Cambridge train.

Plate 64: In 1931, Class D16/2, 4-4-0 'Super Claud' LNER No. 8781 was damaged in an accident near Thorpe-le-Soken. When returned to traffic after repair, it had the modified front end framing that was subsequently used on the piston valve rebuilds. No. 8781, now renumbered BR 62612 and rebuilt to Class D16/3, is seen approaching Haughley on an Ipswich to Norwich train.

Plate 65: Towards the end of steam, three Class K3, 3 cylinder 2-6-0s were stationed at Cambridge to work heavy freight trains to Bletchley and Oxford over the former LNWR line. This picture shows one of these locomotives, No. 61834, working a down freight train near Haughley.

Plate 66: In 1937, two 'Sandringham' Class 3 cylinder 4-6-0s were streamlined, similar to the Gresley A4 Pacifics, in order to work an accelerated express between Norwich and London. The express was called 'The East Anglian' and ran up in the morning and down in the evening. One locomotive was LNER No. 2859 which was renamed *East Anglian* and the other, No. 2870, which was renamed *City of London*. In 1941, in common with all the other streamlined locomotives, the side skirting was removed to ensure easy access to the motion. In 1951 these two locomotives reverted to normal. In this scene, 3 cylinder 4-6-0 Class B17/5, No. 61670 *City of London* is photographed on an Ipswich to Bury St. Edmunds local train in August 1949.

Plate 67: A 'Sandringham' Class, 3 cylinder 4-6-0, No. 61602, *Walsingham* is seen on an up stock train in Haughley station. The stock trains, as they were called, carried empty coaching stock, milk vans, horse boxes and parcels vans, calling at most intermediate stations. This lucrative perishable traffic was the first to be lost to the roads.

Plate 68: A 'Britannia' Class 4-6-2 No. 70011 *Hotspur*, on a down Norwich express, regains the down line at Haughley after single line working from Stowmarket. The ballast train can be seen on the right. On the left is the bay used by the Mid Suffolk Light Railway trains in their last few years. This station replaced the original Light Railway station during the 1939—45 war.

Plate 69: Class K1, 2-6-0 No. 62037 is pictured on the Mid Suffolk Light Railway at Haughley. It had come off the Bury branch with flames pouring from the axle-box of one of the wagons. It was decided to reverse the train up the 1 in 43 bank of the Light Railway, detach the burning wagon and let it run down into the yard. However, no sand was available for No. 62037 when working backwards, so after a magnificent display of slipping the fireman had to get off the footplate and place ballast under the wheels for about a quarter of a mile.

Plate 70: A Class K1, 2-6-0 No. 62017 leaves Haughley on a Cambridge train. The platform to the right was used by the up night mail train from Peterborough. From 1929 until 1969 it connected here with the mail trains from both Liverpool St. and Norwich. The silo had just been completed on what had been the site of the Mid Suffolk Light Railway station. Immediately to the left of the station, in the siding, is a Midland Railway tender which, after rebuilding, had been attached to M&GN 4-4-0 No. 25 *(see Plate 8)*. This tender arrived at Laxfield, newly repainted LNER on 1st January 1948 for use as a water carrier. It survived at Norwich until 1970. On scraping away the more recent coats of paint, the original M&GN golden livery could be exposed beneath in excellent condition. It is interesting that No. 62017 was the locomotive which lost control of its train whilst coming off the Bury branch and eventually crashed into the buffer stops at the end of the loop line.

Plate 71: This photograph, taken on the same afternoon as Plate 70, shows Class K3, 3 cylinder 2-6-0 No. 61801 passing Haughley on a down Norwich express. No. 61801 was, at this time in July 1952, a Stratford 'nominated' locomotive, that is to say a locomotive in excellent condition and fit for express work. It was the second of the class to be built by Gresley at Doncaster in 1920.

Plate 72: A Class J39, 0-6-0 No. 64807 passes Haughley on an up van train. To the right of the picture the track of the Mid Suffolk Light Railway, ascending the 1 in 43 gradient, can be seen.

Plate 73: Mid Suffolk, at the turn of the century, was a remote and sparsely populated area which urgently needed a railway on what are today called social grounds. Professional financiers would have nothing to do with such a scheme so local interests tried to build a DIY railway from Westerfield Junction to Halesworth. They started in 1901 with a sod cutting ceremony by the Duke of Cambridge at Westerfield Junction attended by 601 guests. A sumptuous lunch was greatly enjoyed and two regimental bands provided the music. At this stage in the story, a nebulous Midland Railway tentacle began to emerge hoping to gain access to an East Coast port. The line, therefore, was changed to run from Haughley rather than Westerfield as Haughley was nearer Cambridge, where the Midland line came in from Kettering. No more work was ever done at Westerfield. As was to be expected, a great deal of local money was lost in the building of the line, which never reached beyond Laxfield except for a short freight extension which ran for a few years to Cratfield. This picture shows Class J15, 0-6-0 No. 65447 on a mixed train near Mendlesham with Driver T. Schofield in charge. All the original flat bottomed rail, *(see Plate 34),* had been replaced by 1946 allowing the use of Class J15 0-6-0s in place of the small Class J65 0-6-0 tank locomotives previously employed.

Plate 74 (left above): Class J15, 0-6-0 No. 65408 enters Kenton Junction. The siding in the foreground was part of the proposed line to Westerfield Junction which was laid a couple of miles towards Debenham. Beyond the siding can be seen the water tank fed from a pond which was dug between the two lines. The water was pumped up by a very aged petrol engine. With US Air Force bases in the vicinity, the Mid Suffolk Light Railway fully justified its existence during the 1939—45 war. When the Laxfield train stuck for any reason between Haughley and Kenton, it would be split and the first part placed in the siding at Kenton while the locomotive returned for the rest of the train. Driver G. Rouse is in charge. He had transferred to Suffolk from Yorkshire where he had driven the Beyer-Garratt Class U1, 2-8-8-2, and used to tell of anxious moments on the footplate when the regulator jammed as they were banking flat out at the summit of the Wath incline. He now lives in happy retirement at Laxfield, and is in his early nineties.

Plate 75 (left below): By 1951 the roofs of the old six-wheeled coaches used on the branch had become so porous that, when it was very wet, it was necessary to detach a coach from a passing train at Haughley in order to keep the passengers, mostly schoolchildren, dry. So in October 1951, two sets of two ex-suburban coaches, made redundant by the recent extension of the suburban electrification, arrived at Laxfield hauled by Class J15, 0-6-0 No. 65467. Station Foreman Hubbard is superintending the arrival of the new train. Travel in these coahces, with their straight backs and narrow compartments, was acutely uncomfortable compared with the six-wheelers.

Plate 76 (above): This scene shows the last train from Haughley arriving at Laxfield on 28th July 1952 with detonators exploding beneath Class J15, 0-6-0 No. 65447. Driver Skinner is in charge.

Plate 77 (below): Three days after the closure, Class J15, 0-6-0 No. 65388 came down the branch to pick up any remaining trucks. It is shown here about to leave Laxfield. No. 65388 is fitted with a Darlington-type chimney.

Plate 78: A year later came the demolition trains. This photograph shows Class J15, 0-6-0 No. 65404 near Kenton. It was the last locomotive to work over this section of track which was taken up the next day. Later, in the 1950s and 1960s, demolition trains became a sad and common sight all over East Anglia. Some branches, like the Framlingham branch, were even taken up by road.

Plate 79: From Haughley Junction, the main line ran through Diss to Norwich whilst a long cross-country branch diverged for Bury St. Edmunds, Newmarket, Cambridge and Ely. This picture, taken in 1957, shows a society excursion train which had, earlier in the day, visited Stoke Ferry and Burnham Market coming off the Bury branch at Haughley. It is hauled by Class D16/3, 'Claud Hamilton' 4-4-0 No. 62613. I never again saw a 'Claud Hamilton' 4-4-0 at Haughley.

Plate 80: Class B17/1, 4-6-0 No. 61637 *Thorpe Hall* is seen on a Cambridge to Ipswich train near Bury St. Edmunds.

Plate 81: Bury St. Edmunds was a triple junction. On one side, the branch from Long Melford came in and on the other, the branch from Thetford. The line ahead ran to Newmarket and Cambridge with a branch to Ely diverging at Chippenham Junction, near Newmarket. This view shows Class J17 No. 65528 shunting at Barnham, on the Thetford branch, where there was a large military base in the 1940s and 1950s.

Plate 82: A Class K3, 2-6-0 No. 61971 pilots 'Britannia' Class 4-6-2 No. 70030 *William Wordsworth* on an up express from Norwich. It is passing Thetford West Junction where the branch from Bury St. Edmunds joined the main line. The pilot locomotive was a regular working at that time for operational purposes.

Plate 83: Thetford was on the secondary route from London to Norwich via Ely. On a 'Society Special', 'Britannia' Class 4-6-2 No. 70003 *John Bunyan* passes Two Mile Bottom near Thetford in March 1962.

Plate 84: Class B17/6, 3 cylinder 4-6-0 No. 61626 *Brancepeth Castle* hauls a Yarmouth express at Two Mile Bottom. It is of great interest as the 3rd and 4th coaches, which are articulated, were originally built for the high-speed 'Coronation' express of 1937 which ran from Kings Cross to Edinburgh in six hours.

Plate 85: A branch ran from Thetford to Swaffham which left the Ely to Norwich line at a lonely exchange platform at Roudham Junction. This branch had carried very heavy war-time traffic owing to the service camps at Watton, but in Dr. Beeching's report, it was quoted as the biggest money loser in East Anglia. This was partly due to the fact that the locomotive of the morning school train had to return to Swaffham to change crews. This was done by piloting the branch train and resulted in daily delightful combinations of various locomotives. This scene shows Class C12, 4-4-2T No. 67360, piloted by Class D16/3, 4-4-0 No. 62564 leaving Thetford. The exhaust of the tank locomotive, with its 5 ft. 8 in. driving wheels, contrasted vividly with that of the 4-4-0 with its 7 ft. 0 in. wheels.

Plate 86: This shows an occasion when Class D16/3, 4-4-0 No. 62518 was the train engine and Class J15, 0-6-0 No. 65472 the pilot of the mid-morning Thetford to Swaffham train. The three coaches of the school trains were normally left all day at Thetford. The location is near Roudham Junction.

Plate 87: On 11th August 1968, 'Britannia' Class 4-6-2 No. 70013 *Oliver Cromwell* worked a 'last day of steam' British Railways special from Manchester to Carlisle via Aisgill. No. 70013 then travelled light engine throughout the night to March, where, after a short pause, it continued its journey to Norwich. On 17th August 1968, coupled to the LT&S 4-4-2T No. 80 *Thundersley*, it was hauled to Diss for preservation, in working order, at Bressingham. This picture shows No. 70013 held by signal at Wymondham on 12th August 1968 towards the end of its long journey from Carlisle. The long line of condemned coaches will be noted. These had been bought for scrap by King's of Norwich and were taken two miles down the old Forncett branch to be gutted by fire before being cut up at their Norwich Siding. A member of the North Norfolk Railway used to work overlooking the railway at Wymondham and it is thanks to him that there is such a good collection of old rolling stock at Sheringham.

Plate 88: In 1956, LT&S 4-4-2T No. 80 *Thundersley* was restored to its original condition and made a series of trips to Southend to mark the centenary of the railway. After deteriorating in store for several years, it arrived, unheralded, at Attleborough in 1968 and was locked up in the goods shed. Here, under the guidance of Mr Bill Harvey, the Norwich shed master, it was restored to working order by the Norfolk Railway Society before being hauled to Diss for exhibition in working order at Bressingham. This scene shows the thrilling occasion when, after hours of patient work, *Thundersley* once again worked a van up and down the siding under its own steam.

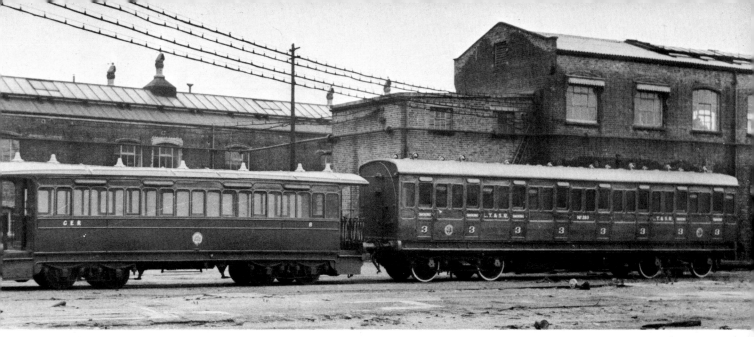

Plate 89: For the centenary trips to Southend an old LT&S coach was carefully restored, which finally found its way to Stratford. This coach is seen attached to GER bogie coach No. 8. The GER coach was built in 1884 for the Wisbech & Upwell Tramway. When this branch was closed to passenger traffic in 1929, the coach was transferred to the Kelvedon and Tollesbury branch. It provided a most uncomfortable ride, like the Southwold Railway coaches. One had to sit with one's back to the windows, though there was more room for one's legs. No. 8 became famous, being used in the film 'The Titfield Thunderbolt'. It is seen here in 1957 when it was intended to preserve both coaches. Unfortunately both were shortly afterwards damaged beyond repair.

Plate 90: Returning to Bury St. Edmunds, near Kennett, Class L1, 2-6-4T No. 67709 pilots Class B12/3, 4-6-0 No. 61537 on a local train from Cambridge. This was a regular double-headed working.

Plate 91: Beyond Kennett, the line continues to Cambridge via Newmarket and before Newmarket is reached, a line for Ely branches off at Chippenham Junction. There was also a spur from Warren Hill, Newmarket, to the Ely line at Snailwell Junction. This spur was used by the once very lucrative racehorse traffic from Newmarket to the north and also to turn the LNER Pacifics used on the Newmarket 'Race Specials' from Kings Cross during the 1930s. At Fordham Junction, on the line to Ely, a branch line came in from Cambridge and diverged at once for Mildenhall. This scene shows Class 2-6-0 No. 46467 near Burwell, on the Mildenhall branch, hauling a Sunday excursion train to Hunstanton.

Plate 92: Class B1, 4-6-0 No. 61254 shunts at Barway Crossing on the single track section between Soham and Ely. The old GER signal with a slotted post is being replaced. The loop line at Barway Crossing was signalled for use in either direction and saw extensive use throughout the 1939—45 war.

Plate 93: Ely is the first big junction going north from Cambridge. To the south, a branch line came in from St. Ives on which passenger traffic ceased in 1930. When London was badly bombed during the 1939—45 war, the yards at Cambridge soon became choked. Vital traffic was then sent to East Anglia, via the Midland route from Kettering to St. Ives. Here the small Midland 0-6-0s ran round their trains and worked tender-first to Ely with a Cambridge pilotman. Class 2-6-0 No. 46466 is seen at Sutton, on the St. Ives to Ely branch, on a Sunday excursion train to Hunstanton.

Plate 94: A Class J15, 0-6-0 No. 65457 leaves Wilburton station on the Ely to Sutton section. During the sugar beet season, this small country station dealt with a large volume of traffic but, unfortunately, for about nine months of the year towards the end of the 1950s, it was virtually unused.

Plate 95: A Class K1, 2-6-0 No. 62055 hauls a southbound freight train, taking the Ely station avoiding line en route for Bury St. Edmunds.

Plate 96: At Ely North Junction, the line divides into three, to the right it runs to Thetford and Norwich, ahead, it proceeds to Dereham and King's Lynn and to the left it runs to March. An Ely avoiding loop makes it possible for trains to run direct from March to Dereham and from March to Norwich. This view shows a Midland Region Class 4, 0-6-0 No. 44509 on a short freight train at March. On the right is one of the early Class 31 diesels. The decline in coal traffic has seen a corresponding decline in the importance of March as a rail centre. With the proposed total closure of the joint line from March to Spalding, it would seem that, as a railway centre, March will soon become a small country halt.

Plate 97: This picture, taken in May 1960, shows Class B17/6, 3 cylinder 4-6-0 No. 61657 *Doncaster Rovers* fitted with a boiler pressed to 225 lb per sq. inch. Behind it is Class B17/4, 3 cylinder 4-6-0 No. 61660 still fitted with an original boiler pressed to 180 lb per sq. inch. On the introduction of the new diesel locomotives in 1959, No. 61660 had been put into store at Lowestoft, and as it was not then intended to use it again, its name plates *Hull City* were handed over to the football club of that name. However, owing to the teething troubles of the diesels, it was necessary to return No. 61660 to traffic at March. Here, *Borstal* 'Schools Class', was very neatly painted on the splasher to which the name plates had been attached. Nos. 61657 and 61660 were both withdrawn a few weeks later.

Plate 98: This photograph shows Class B1, 4-6-0 No. 61258 with a self-weighing tender. It is working a local train over the GN & GE Joint line from March to Lincoln and Doncaster. It is shown crossing the M & GN line on the level at Murrow.

Plate 99: In this scene, 2-10-0 No. 92195 hauls an Immingham to Thames Haven bulk chemical train at Murrow. If only LMS outside-framed 2-4-0 No. 20012 could have survived for a few more years, what a photograph it would have made standing side by side with a BR 2-10-0 and Bill Last standing between them.

Plate 100: The scene is a pouring wet Sunday, on the occasion of a 'Society Special' to Benwick, the terminus of a freight-only branch which left the March to Peterborough line at Three Horse Shoes Junction. The locomotive is Class J17 No. 65562. According to local gossip, occasional excursion trains had been run from Benwick in the past but I never found any positive confirmation of this. After travelling back in the open trucks to Whittlesea, the 'Society Special' proceeded to Wisbech where a train of more open trucks was waiting. Here, in even heavier rain, the society travelled over the tram-way to Outwell and back, at the regulation speed of 12 m.p.h. I shall never forget the incredulous look on the faces of passing motorists as they saw this extraordinary train load of people, apparently thoroughly enjoying themselves.

Plate 101: A Class D16/3, 4-4-0 No. 62606 passes Wiggenhall siding on a March to King's Lynn train. From the reversed nameboard over the buffer beam, one of its duties that day must have been 'The Fenman'.

Plate 102: With a train from March, Class B17/6, 4-6-0 No. 61621 *Hatfield House* approaches King's Lynn.

Plate 103: This view shows Class B17/6, 3 cylinder 4-6-0 No. 61640 *Somerleyton Hall* leaving King's Lynn on a Hunstanton express. A 'Sandringham' with a small tender could be turned both at King's Lynn and Hunstanton, whereas a large-tendered 'Football' could not.

Plate 104: Class D16/3, 4-4-0 No. 62588 was one of ten 'Claud Hamiltons' to be rebuilt with 8in. piston valves. It is seen here leaving King's Lynn on a Hunstanton train.

Plate 105: A Class D16/3, 4-4-0 No. 62543 leaves King's Lynn on an up Cambridge and Liverpool St. express. In the early-1950s, fourteen trains were booked to run to Hunstanton on summer Sunday mornings, and in addition, there were always a few extra specials. The working of this intensive train service, over the single track from Wolferton to Hunstanton, was fascinating to watch. Whilst most trains were hauled by 'Claud Hamilton' Class D16/3, 4-4-0s, a great variety of locomotives was used such as Class L1, 2-6-4 tanks, LMS 'Crab' 2-6-0s and LMS Class 4, 0-6-0s.

Plate 106: A small Class J69, 0-6-0 tank was rarely seen on an express duty but, on this occasion, No. 68566 had worked a 'Society Special' to Stoke Ferry taking over from Class B12/3, 4-6-0 No. 61577 at Denver Junction. It then worked back express to King's Lynn and is seen approaching this location.

Plate 107: In view of the extensive sand traffic from Middleton Towers, on the line from King's Lynn to Dereham, it is surprising that no run-round facilities were ever installed there. The three daily trains of empty trucks had always, therefore, to be double-headed from King's Lynn, unless they ran on to East Winch, the next station. In this scene, Class J17, 0-6-0 No. 65549 is shown piloting another locomotive of the same class. The departure of trains with empty trucks from King's Lynn was always a dramatic sight. Later, special wagons were provided for this traffic as the trucks had to be scrupulously clean.

Plate 108 (right upper): A Class J69, 0-6-0T No. 68498, seen at Middleton Towers in June 1958, is one of the locomotives ▷ which had brought the train of empty trucks from King's Lynn and which is keeping safely out of the way whilst shunting is in progress. The works tank engine *Peter*, Hudswell Clarke No. 1640 of 1929, is taking the empty trucks up to the factory for loading. Note the man cleaning the trucks on the left and the watering cans which hang from them.

Plate 109 (right lower): Beyond Middleton Towers, the line ran to Swaffham and Dereham. At Swaffham the branch came ▷ in from Thetford. In this picture, taken in May 1961, Class B12/3, 4-6-0 No. 61572, the last of the class in service, is shown at Swaffham about to work a 'school special' over the Thetford branch to Liverpool St. Including the empty coaching stock working to and from Norwich via the Dereham avoiding curve, the day's trip for 61572 covered over 300 miles. No. 61572 was finally withdrawn in September 1961 and is now being reconditioned by the North Norfolk Railway at Sheringham.

Plate 110: A Class J19, 0-6-0 No. 64643 and a Class J17, 0-6-0 standing at the buffers at Dereham. The very fine GER signals add interest to the scene.

Plate 112: Also at Dereham, one of the last rebuilt 'Claud Hamilton' Class D16/3, 4-4-0s to remain in service, No. 62544, works the North Elmham to Norwich milk train.

Plate 111: In this picture, taken in August 1952, the last D15 unrebuilt 'Claud Hamilton' 4-4-0 to remain in service, No. 62509, is shown a few weeks before its withdrawal. It was built at Stratford in 1900 and is seen on a Dereham to King's Lynn train at Dereham station.

Plate 113: Beyond Dereham the line ran to Fakenham and Wells-next-the-Sea. At County School a branch diverged to Wroxham on the Norwich to Cromer line. This view shows Class J19, 0-6-0 No. 64674 working a sugar beet train from Foulsham which had, by the time this picture was taken, become the terminus of the branch. Before the closure of the County School to Wroxham branch in 1952, it was possible to take a cheap day ticket from Norwich to Foulsham for 17p, (in today's money). One went out to Wymondham on the main line behind a Class E4, 2-4-0 and then to Dereham and County School on the Wells-next-the-sea branch. At County School, one cut across Norfolk through Foulsham and Aylsham to Wroxham and then back to Norwich on the Cromer line. On arrival at Norwich, another Class E4, 2-4-0 backed on to the train and repeated the whole circle. I once met a fellow passenger who said it was his third time round and all for 17p. It was a pity the line had to be closed due to lack of financial support.

Plate 114: Returning to the Ipswich to Norwich main line which was left at Haughley, this scene shows a Norwich to Stowmarket local train, hauled by Class K3, 2-6-0 No. 61957, refuged at Diss to allow it to be overtaken by a London express. This was a daily working requiring the points to be locked by hand by the signalman.

Plate 115: An up East Anglian express climbs to Norwich Trowse Upper Junction behind 'Britannia' Class 4-6-2 No. 70012 *John of Gaunt.*

Plate 116: In this view a down express is seen at Trowse Upper Junction hauled by 'Britannia' Class 4-6-2 No. 70040 *Clive of India.*

Plate 117: The Eastern Union Railway's line from Ipswich to Norwich opened in 1849 and its terminus was at Norwich Victoria. In 1851, the Eastern Union Railway built the connecting line from Norwich Trowse Upper Junction to the Eastern Counties line at Trowse Lower Junction. Most trains from Ipswich, thereafter, ran to Norwich Thorpe but a few continued to use Norwich Victoria until 1916 when it became a goods depot. It is now a coal concentration yard. This scene shows Class K3, 3 cylinder 2-6-0 No. 61971 working a Whitemoor, March to Norwich freight train on to the Victoria branch at Trowse Upper Junction. It is being banked by Class J69, 0-6-0T No. 68555.

Plate 118: To reach Trowse Upper Junction, freight trains from Whitemoor had to reverse at Trowse Lower Junction where a pilot locomotive was attached to the rear of the train. This picture shows the pilot locomotive, Class J69, 0-6-0T No. 68555, climbing the bank. This locomotive had spent twenty years in Scotland and was thus very much in its original GER condition. At the rear can be seen the smoke of the train engine, Class K3, 3 cylinder 2-6-0 No. 61971, shown also in the previous photograph. To hear the two locomotives pounding their way up the bank on a still day was one of the best railway sounds in East Anglia.

Plate 119: A 4-6-2 'Britannia', No. 70007 *Coeur-de-Lion* hauls, on the Norwich Victoria branch, a freight train from Whitemoor. It had reversed both at Trowse Lower Junction and Trowse Upper Junction. The pilot locomotive, attached to the rear of the train at Trowse Lower Junction, is now banking.

Plate 120: When, after their introduction in 1951, 'Britannias' were not available for the Norwich expresses, a Class B1 4-6-0 made a very able substitute. However, this required very skilful driving to keep to the time schedule with a heavy train. This scene shows Class B1, 4-6-0 No. 61227 descending the bank from Trowse Upper Junction with the down 'Norfolkman' express.

Plate 121: 'Britannia' Class 4-6-2 No. 70041 *Sir John Moore* ascends the bank to Trowse Upper Junction on the up 'East Anglian' express.

Plate 122: As no 'Britannia' had been available for this up express, a Norwich Class B1, 4-6-0 No. 61317 was deputising and is seen passing Trowse Lower Junction, tackling the bank. Part of the charm of a steam locomotive was that, at times, in good condition and with a good crew, it could produce results which were theoretically impossible, a human attribute missing from the diesels.

Plate 123: A Class B1, 4-6-0 No. 61043 passes Trowse Lower Junction signal box on a down express. Class B1, 4-6-0 locomotives Nos. 1040—1052 were sent to Norwich in 1946 on being built by the North British Locomotive Company, and Nos. 1053—1059 were sent to Ipswich. These twenty locomotives were regarded as the best B1s on the Eastern Region.

Plate 124: Civil Engineer's departmental locomotive No. 39 could always be seen shunting the Engineer's yard outside Norwich. It was a Sentinel type locomotive and was kept in spotless condition.

Plate 125: The line ran eastwards from Norwich Thorpe to Whitlingham Junction where the lines to Cromer and Yarmouth divided. Because of the complexity of the local train service, all trains in and out of Norwich Thorpe carried a local route-indicating headcode. This photograph shows Class N7/3, 0-6-2T No. 69708 on a Yarmouth Vauxhall to Norwich, via Reedham Junction, train near Whitlingham Junction. The recess in the cab side, for holding the M&GN Whitaker staff pick-up apparatus, can clearly be seen.

Plate 126: A Norwich to Yarmouth Vauxhall, via Acle, train passes Whitlingham Junction hauled by Class N7/3, 0-6-2T No. 69707. During the 1950s, Norwich had about half a dozen of these essentially London suburban locomotives and they carried out a great deal of work of all kinds.

Plate 127: After the war, the very variegated collection of old locomotives, that had been working on the M&GN section, were largely replaced by new Ivatt LMS type 4MT 2-6-0s. This picture shows such a locomotive, No. 43151, stationed at Melton Constable, approaching Whitlingham Junction on a Cromer to Norwich train.

Plate 128: The Cromer line started climbing, for two miles, immediately on leaving Whitlingham Junction. The first mile was as steep as 1 in 80. This view shows 3 cylinder Class B17/6, 4-6-0 No. 61665 *Leicester City* starting the climb with an eleven coach train. In these days of the universal d.m.u., the heavy tasks performed by the steam locomotives are now a cause for surprise.

Plate 129: This photograph shows Class B1, 4-6-0 No. 61042 approaching Whitlingham Junction on an up Cromer express. Some trains, such as the 'Holiday Camps Express', from Liverpool St. to Caister-on-Sea, were non-stop to and from Wroxham, via Ely. These trains stopped for water at Brandon. A post-war proposal, which came to nothing, was for the laying of water troughs at Brandon.

Plate 130 (right): A Class B12/3, 4-6-0 No. 61547 tackles the 1 in 80 gradient up from Whitlingham Junction on a down Cromer express. Because of the curve, this bank could not be rushed.

Plate 131 (below): The lines around Cromer were so lavish and complex that one wonders if their construction had not been influenced by the fears of a German invasion of East Anglia so prevalent at the end of the last century. Cromer was first reached by the GER in 1877, its terminus, Cromer High, being situated on top of a hill one mile from the town. Passenger services ceased in 1954 and freight services in 1960. This view shows Class B1, 4-6-0 No. 61204 shunting at Cromer High immediately prior to its complete closure. It was taken to show how the line ran above the house and hotel.

Plate 132: In 1887 the railway from Melton Constable reached Cromer Beach, a station much more centrally situated than Cromer High. This line became part of the M&GN in 1893. In 1898 the North Walsham to Mundesley line was opened. This was extended to Cromer Beach in 1906 by the Norfolk & Suffolk Joint Committee, a committee composed of GER and M&GN railway members. At the same time, in 1906, a line was opened from Cromer Junction, just under a mile from Cromer High, to Roughton Road Junction, on the Mundesley to Cromer Beach branch. At this time, a loop was also built from Newstead Lane Junction, on the same line, to Runton West Junction on the Melton Constable to Cromer Beach branch. This view shows Class N7/3, 0-6-2T No. 69679 leaving Cromer Junction with through coaches from Liverpool St. to Sheringham. These had been detached from the Cromer High train at Cromer Junction box. This mode of operation was employed for the Sheringham coaches of the down 'Norfolk Coast Express'.

Plate 133: At other times, through coaches for Sheringham would be taken into Cromer High and then propelled out again to Cromer Junction before proceeding to Sheringham. This scene shows a Class B17/3, 3 cylinder 4-6-0 No. 61665 *Leicester City* propelling its train for Sheringham from Cromer High up to Cromer Junction box where it will reverse. The locomotive has been turned, as there was no turntable at Sheringham. In the reverse direction all trains from Sheringham had to reverse at Cromer Junction and be propelled into Cromer High. This was an unusual and always fascinating movement. Quite high speeds were attained and it always looked, if you leaned out of the window, as if the train would go over the edge at the end of the station.

Plate 134: Cromer High was closed to passengers in 1954 and trains were diverted to Cromer Beach. This picture, taken soon after the closure, shows Class B17/6, 3 cylinder 4-6-0 No. 61654 *Sunderland* climbing with a London express from the former Roughton Road Junction to Cromer Junction. The line from Roughton Road Junction to Mundesley had been closed in 1953.

Plate 135: A London express from Cromer Beach takes the loop between Runton East Junction and Newstead Lane Junction and is hauled by Class B12/3, 4-6-0 No. 61540 piloting a Class A5, 4-6-2T No. 69826. The loop from Newstead Lane Junction to Runton West Junction, which enabled trains to run through direct from Cromer Junction to Sheringham, is shown in the foreground. The line from Cromer Beach to Sheringham is in the background, on the left.

Plate 136: This scene shows Class B1, 4-6-0 No. 61399 passing Runton West Junction box, in October 1959, hauling a Norwich Thorpe to Norwich City freight on an occasion when it had been routed via Cromer Beach in order to detach some wagons. This very round about route was made necessary by the closure of nearly all the M&GN section in February 1959. In September 1960, the Themelthorpe curve was opened which enabled these trains to run via Lenwade and Wroxham, a considerably shorter distance. The line to the right of the picture is that shown in the foreground of the previous photograph, and runs from Runton West Junction to Newstead Lane Junction. The Newstead Lane to Cromer Beach line can be seen in the background.

Plate 137: A Class B12/3, 4-6-0 No. 61533 hauls a Liverpool St. to Sheringham through train and approaches Runton West Junction box. It had reversed at Cromer Beach.

Plate 138: The previous picture shows such an apparently large junction that it is hard to believe that this photograph was obtained merely by crossing from one side of the overbridge to the other. It shows Class B17/3, 3 cylinder 4-6-0 No. 61636 *Harlaxton Manor* on a Melton Constable to Cromer Beach train approaching Runton West Junction box. Trains here made a lovely sight with the sea shimmering in the background. The best sight of all, however, was at Cromer Links Halt where, in late summer, the train from North Walsham would suddenly burst out on to a hillside, high above the sea, which was covered with heather.

Plate 139: A Class B17/6, 3 cylinder 4-6-0 No. 61654 *Sunderland* enters Melton Constable in 1959 on a Norwich Thorpe to Norwich City freight train. Melton Constable Works was, at this time, employed in breaking up old wagons.

Plate 140: The main M&GN line ran from Melton Constable to Yarmouth Beach via North Walsham. This picture shows an Ivatt LMS type Class 4, 2-6-0 No. 43155 on a local train leaving North Walsham. In the background, on the Cromer line, can be seen the stock of the North Walsham school train. A train from Cromer is signalled.

Plate 141: A Class J39, 0-6-0 No. 64900 leaves Aylsham (M&GN) on a freight train.

Plate 142: Before leaving the Norwich area, it would seem appropriate to mention the firm of King's, who bought, for scrap, large numbers of steam locomotives and coaches made redundant by the introduction of the diesels. Great Western 'Counties', 'Castles', 'Halls', 'Moguls', 2-6-2 tanks, large and small 2-8-0s, Collett 0-6-0s, 2-8-0 tanks, 2-8-2 tanks and 0-6-0 Pannier tanks came to the scrapyard at Norwich. Class Q and Q1 Austerity 0-6-0s came from the Southern Region, together with 2 and 3 cylinder 2-6-0s both with 5ft. 6in. and 6ft. 0in. driving wheels and three LBSC Class K 2-6-0s. One Class H Wainwright 0-4-4T also arrived from the Southern. Class A1 and A3 Pacifics were the most interesting locomotives from the LNER. This picture shows LBSC Class K 2-6-0 No. 32343, two GWR Collett 0-6-0s and a GWR 2-6-2T awaiting cutting up in King's sidings at Trowse Upper Junction. It is interesting to record that the Brighton 2-6-0s were made of such good steel that they were by far the most difficult locomotives to cut up from all those that came to Norwich. I was told that cutting up a post-war GWR 'Castle' was like cutting up tissue paper when compared with a pre-war example.

Plate 143: At Whitlingham Junction, a Class J39, 0-6-0 No. 64802 leaves on a Yarmouth Vauxhall, via Acle, train. The J39s were extensively used on all types of traffic during the 1930s when they were new. They were largely replaced on passenger work in East Anglia during the 1950s by Class K3, 3 cylinder 2-6-0s. A Class J39 0-6-0 was once recorded as travelling at 73 m.p.h. on a down Norwich express near Diss, registering 70 m.p.h. on two other occasions on the journey from Ipswich.

Plate 144: A Class B1, 4-6-0 No. 61050 passes Whitlingham Junction on a through summer Saturday train from Yarmouth to the Midlands. This train would take both the Norwich and Ely avoiding curves.

Plate 145: A Yarmouth Vauxhall to Norwich train comes off the Acle line, at Brundall, behind Class D16/3, 4-4-0 No. 62613.

Plate 146: With the Yarmouth portion of the through train from York, a Class K3, 3 cylinder 2-6-0 No. 61957 leaves Reedham Junction. Class L1, 2-6-4T No. 67736 waits in the siding to back on to the Lowestoft coaches.

Plate 147 (top): A Class A5, 4-6-2T No. 69824 passes Reedham Junction with a freight train bound for Lowestoft. The train is largely composed of conflats, the forerunners of the modern freightliner wagons.

Plate 148 (left): The stock of the up morning train from Yarmouth South Town, via the East Suffolk line, returned to Norwich via the main line through Diss. It was then worked back to Yarmouth South Town as empty coaching stock, via Lowestoft, where it reversed, and Gorleston. This picture shows Class D16/3, 4-4-0 No. 62511, originally built at Stratford in 1901, working the empty coaching stock through Haddiscoe.

Plate 149 (bottom): The fish traffic from Lowestoft, particularly herrings, had always been an important source of revenue for the Great Eastern Railway. This view shows a Class B1, 4-6-0 No. 61043 picking up fish vans from the harbour before leaving for Norwich on a local train.

Plate 150: In 1847, Yarmouth's first connection by rail with Lowestoft was via Reedham Junction. In 1872, a spur was put in at Haddiscoe to shorten the journey and finally, in 1903, the Norfolk & Suffolk Joint Committee built the direct coast line via Gorleston. Like the North Walsham to Cromer line constructed by the same committee, it was built on a very lavish scale. This scene shows a Class F5, 2-4-2T No. 67199 working a Yarmouth South Town to Lowestoft push and pull train leaving Gorleston. No. 67199 is carrying, most unusually, a 30D (Southend Victoria) shed plate. Trains from Lowestoft to Yarmouth Beach diverged at Gorleston North Junction and then crossed the Breydon viaduct.

Plate 151: Traffic on the Yarmouth to Lowestoft coast line never reached expectations and it was only busy on summer Saturdays. This scene shows a Class D16/3, 4-4-0 No. 62570, near Hopton, working a summer Saturday holiday train from Gorleston. After reversal at Lowestoft, this train made a non-stop run up to Liverpool St. behind an Ipswich Class B12/3, 4-6-0 locomotive.

Plate 152: Pictured in 1960, this scene shows a rare and interesting working of a Class L1, 2-6-4T No. 67738 working a Yarmouth South Town to Liverpool St. express near Lowestoft North, over the coast line. These trains were, at this time, usually diesel hauled. In February 1959 Yarmouth had been hit by the complete closure of the M&GN section and in December 1959 it was hit again by the complete closure of the direct line from Yarmouth South Town to Beccles. For a time some trains were diverted, as seen in this photograph, via Lowestoft but owing to passenger resistance to increased mileage and thus higher fares, the service was soon withdrawn. Work had been started on bringing the coast line up to main line standards but this was soon stopped. The line was first singled and then finally closed in 1970. All this had been correctly foreseen by local railwaymen who maintained that there was a natural traffic flow between Ipswich and Yarmouth over the East Suffolk line, but not between Ipswich and Lowestoft. They saw that some reorganization of routes was necessary and their solution was to keep the 1926 swing bridge at Beccles in operation and divert Yarmouth trains over the original 1854 route from Halesworth to Norwich via Haddiscoe. At Reedham Junction all that was then required was the relaying of the avoiding curve. Lowestoft traffic would have had to change trains at Haddiscoe. The Reedham avoiding curve had, apparently, last been used in 1926 when St. Olaves bridge was being renewed.

Plate 153: This scene shows the Yarmouth South Town to Lowestoft push and pull train approaching Coke Ovens Junction, Lowestoft, (a reminder of the very early days of railways when locomotives burnt coke and not coal), behind Class N7/2, 0-6-2T No. 69689.

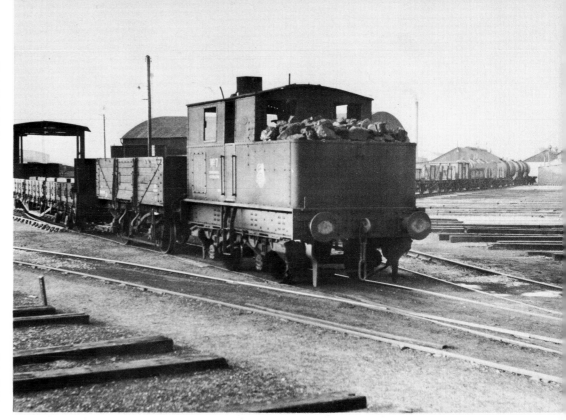

Plate 154: Sentinel departmental locomotive No. 7 carries out shunting duties in the sleeper factory at Lowestoft. The timber from Scandinavia was unloaded on to the quay and processed in the factory on the spot.

Plate 155: A down express approaches Lowestoft hauled by 'Britannia' Class 4-6-2 No. 70000 *Britannia*. The line to the sleeper factory is shown in the foreground.

Plate 156: This scene shows Class F6, 2-4-2T No. 67224 working through coaches from Lowestoft to Liverpool St. at Oulton Broad North Junction. They would be attached to the train from Yarmouth at Beccles.

Plate 157: A vacuum fitted Class J17, 0-6-0 No. 65558 stands at Lowestoft South Harbour. This was a delightful railway backwater entirely untouched by the march of progress.

Plate 158 (top): Once the pride of Ipswich shed, Class B1, 4-6-0 No. 61059 crosses St. Olaves swing bridge at Haddiscoe. The 1872 loop to Lowestoft diverged in the immediate foreground.

Plate 159 (bottom): A Class K3, 3 cylinder 2-6-0 No. 61973 works a freight train at Haddiscoe over the line to Fleet Junction which was taken, between 1854 and 1859, by trains from Norwich to Halesworth. The line from Haddiscoe to Yarmouth South Town was not built until 1859. Haddiscoe signal box, seen to the left of the picture, is now an exhibit at the South Kensington Science Museum.

Plate 160: 'Britannia' Class 4-6-2 No. 70037 *Hereward the Wake* leaves Beccles for Yarmouth on the down 'Easterling' express. This train ran in the 1950s, during the summer months, non-stop from Liverpool St. to Beccles where the Yarmouth and Lowestoft portions were divided.

Plate 161: In this view the Lowestoft coaches, off the 'Easterling' express, leave Beccles behind Class F6, 2-4-2T No. 67223.

Plate 162: This picture shows Class N7/3, 0-6-2T No. 69679 approaching Beccles on the Yarmouth South Town to Beccles push and pull train.

Plate 163: Beccles was a triple junction with the line to Lowestoft diverging to the right and the Waveney Valley branch to Tivetshall to the left. This scene shows Class B12/3, 4-6-0 No. 61535 on the Waveney Valley branch at Bungay, in January 1952, with the Ipswich steam crane. A violent autumn gale had blown down so many trees on the neighbouring estates that the goods yard had become choked up with them, and the small travelling crane, seen behind the dome of the locomotive on view, was unable to cope. This crane was still lettered M&GN, although the M&GN had ceased to exist over fifteen years earlier. This is a very rare photograph as only Class J15, 0-6-0s, Class E4, 2-4-0s and Class F4 and F5 2-4-2 tanks were normally allowed to cross the weak bridge at Beccles. The heavier locomotives often used on the Harleston goods train always reversed there. No. 61535 had reached Bungay via Tivetshall. As recounted in Richard Hardy's book, *Steam in the Blood*, No. 61535 had run into difficulties whilst working the down mail one very wintry night, in January 1952, and this was its first running in trip after repair.

Plate 164: A Class J15, 0-6-0 No. 65471 works a freight train near Homersfield, with sugar beet destined for the factory at Cantley.

Plate 165 (top): A 'society special' approaches Homersfield behind Class J15, 0-6-0 No. 65469.

Plate 166 (middle): The up morning train leaves Halesworth behind two Class B12/3, 4-6-0s, Nos. 61561 and 61564. The down morning paper train had no return working so the locomotive usually returned to Ipswich as pilot, as in the photograph.

Plate 167 (bottom): In the final days of steam, in 1960, a very interesting locomotive working was instituted over the East Suffolk line. On the first day, a freight train would be worked from March to Lowestoft via Norwich and after spending the night at Lowestoft, the locomotive worked to Ipswich over the East Suffolk line and then returned to March via Bury St. Edmunds in the evening. This working brought many strangers to the area, like 'Austerity' 2-8-0 No. 90709, shown in this scene at Halesworth.

Plate 168 (above): Another rare locomotive on this duty was Class 01, 2-8-0 No. 63687 also pictured at Halesworth.

Plate 169 (below): On this occasion, the usual March locomotive had been replaced on the up goods by Norwich Class K3, 3 cylinder 2-6-0 No. 61989. The up afternoon express is seen leaving Halesworth behind 'Britannia' Class 4-6-2 No. 70000 *Britannia*, with No. 61989 standing nearby in the goods shed.

Plate 170: Another Norwich Class K3, 3 cylinder 2-6-0 No. 61949 climbs away from Halesworth. The line had originally been constructed very cheaply, involving a few earthworks. There were thus many level crossings which have become increasingly expensive to maintain. The Mid Suffolk Light Railway was originally intended to reach Halesworth at the bottom of the gradient to the extreme right of this picture.

Plate 171: 'Britannia' Class 4-6-2 No. 70035 *Rudyard Kipling* approaches the summit of the bank out of Halesworth with the up afternoon express. During the previous week I had been granted a footplate pass from Liverpool St. to Norwich and back and No. 70035 was the locomotive on which I had travelled down. This was a red letter day I shall never forget, the trip being so much better in fact than was anticipated, which is saying a great deal. Having met the inspector who was to accompany me, there followed that exquisite moment, over all too soon, of climbing up on to the footplate knowing that one could stay there for the next two hours. Waiting for the train to start, I thought about all the articles I had ever read concerning cut-offs and regulator openings. However, once the train started, there was no time for such things whilst revelling in the sheer enjoyment of such an experience. The locomotive pounded away and every time the fireman opened the firebox door there was the sight of the roaring furnace.

At times one suddenly came back to earth, like when we passed a vixen with her cubs sunning themselves on the railway bank near Ilford. All the time the driver's attention was fixed on the track ahead. At Needham Market we came to a stop at an adverse signal caused by a diesel locomotive which had failed. The driver then relaxed and gave me his opinion of the diesels. When we got the signal to go, he was away again, determined that our lateness into Norwich should be as little as possible. Once over the summit at Haughley, the locomotive began to pulsate more and more, every single thing on it becoming alive, until finally the speedometer touched 94 m.p.h. as we tore through the station at Diss. A few minutes later we seemed to be going so slowly that I looked again at the speedometer; it was showing only 80 m.p.h. Returning on No. 70013 *Oliver Cromwell* we set off well. However, I noticed that the boiler pressure was beginning to fall. It continued to fall, faster and faster, but not a word was spoken. The driver looked at the track ahead, the inspector looked at the fireman, and the fireman looked at his fire. The inspector took off his jacket, got the pricker off the tender and with the locomotive still roaring away, attended to the fire. After what seemed a very long time, the needle on the pressure gauge stopped falling and, with the fireman building up his fire, it began to rise once more. There was, therefore, no need to come off the train at Ipswich. This photograph brings back vivid memories of that occasion.

Plate 172 (left middle): Class J20, 0-6-0 No. 64690, not in the best of condition, is making heavy weather of the climb out of Halesworth as it approaches the summit. Class J20s were very rare visitors to the East Suffolk line.

Plate 173 (left bottom): With an up afternoon freight train, Class B1, 4-6-0 No. 61227, with electrified wire warning plates, leaves Darsham.

Plate 174 (right): The up morning train, which usually carried express headlights, leaves Darsham behind Class B12/3, 4-6-0 No. 61561 piloting Class B1, 4-6-0 No. 61252.

Plate 175: This scene shows the up morning train near Saxmundham, hauled by Class B17/1, 3 cylinder 4-6-0 No. 61629 *Naworth Castle* piloting Class B17/1, 4-6-0 No. 61621 *Hatfield House*. Both locomotives were, at that time, fitted with the original 180 lb boilers.

Plate 176: A Class B1, 4-6-0 No. 61311 is seen working an Ipswich to Yarmouth slow train near Saxmundham. Colchester locomotives did not usually work down the East Suffolk line and at this time, No. 61311 was Colchester's 'black sheep' usually to be seen as station pilot or on the breakdown train.

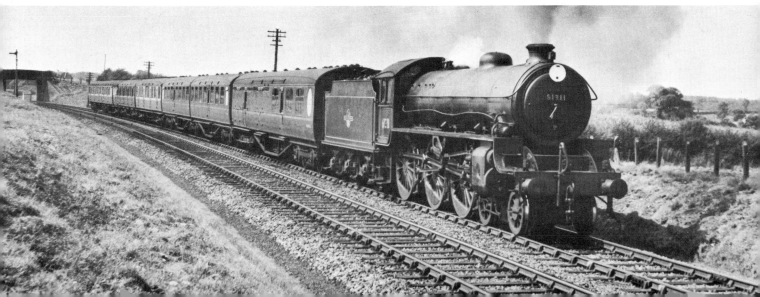

Plate 177: Class B12/3, 4-6-0 No. 61572 works a down slow train near Saxmundham. No. 61572 is now preserved by the North Norfolk Railway and is being reconditioned at Sheringham.

Plate 178: On temporary loan from Norwich to Yarmouth South Town, Class K3, 3 cylinder 2-6-0 No. 61970 leaves Saxmundham on a down train. Class J15, 0-6-0 No. 65447 waits to reverse into the station before proceeding to Aldeburgh. Diesel multiple units took over the branch working the following week.

Plate 179: This atmospheric scene shows Class B12/3, 4-6-0 No. 61571 climbing away from Saxmundham Junction on an Aldeburgh branch train.

Plate 180: At Leiston, the shunter at Garrett's works, as shown in this photograph, was an Aveling & Porter locomotive named *Sirapite*, now preserved by Sir William McAlpine. It is of interest that parts of the bodywork of the Class 31 diesel locomotive were manufactured at Leiston works.

Plate 181: At Snape Junction, a short branch ran down to the Maltings, now a world famous concert centre. This picture shows Class J15, 0-6-0 No. 65459 on the branch, passing the Snape Junction fixed distant signal.

Plate 183: The 1 in 53 gradient down from Snape Junction to Snape is evident in this photograph of 'Britannia' Class 4-6-2 No. 70038 *Robin Hood* passing the junction on an up express.

Plate 182: In 1956, Class E4, 2-4-0 No. 61797 worked a 'society special' down to Snape. This is believed to have been the only occasion on which a passenger train reached there. Class E4 No. 62797 propelled its train back to the junction but was held by signal, on the 1 in 53 gradient, to allow the Halesworth milk train to pass. It was unable to restart and Class J15, 0-6-0 No. 65447 was sent down to assist.

Plate 184 (right above): A 'Britannia' Class 4-6-2 No. 70035 *Rudyard Kipling* is pictured working an up slow train past Snape Junction.

Plate 185 (right middle): Class B17/6, 3 cylinder 4-6-0 No. 61618 *Wynyard Park* passes Snape Junction with the down morning stock train. The empty milk tanks were destined for Halesworth.

Plate 186 (right bottom): The up afternoon stock train, with the Halesworth milk tanks now full, is shown passing Snape Junction behind Class B17/6, 3 cylinder 4-6-0 No. 61672 *West Ham United*.

Plate 187: In this rural scene, Class B17/6, 3 cylinder 4-6-0 No. 61611 *Raynham Hall* hauls an up Yarmouth express near Wickham Market Junction.

Plate 188: With 'Britannia' Class 4-6-2 No. 70039 *Sir Christopher Wren* in charge, a down express passes Wickham Market Junction.

Plate 189: No. 61566, a 4-6-0 Class B12/3 locomotive, passes Wickham Market Junction with a down slow train.

Plate 190: Class B12/3, 4-6-0 No. 61535 belches black smoke as it hauls the down morning stock train whilst passing Wickham Market Junction.

Plate 191: At Wickham Market Junction the up morning train recovers from a signal check, on this occasion powered by Class B17/6, 3 cylinder 4-6-0 No. 61622 *Alnwick Castle* piloted by Class B17/1, 3 cylinder 4-6-0 No. 61637 *Thorpe Hall*.

Plate 192: A Class B1, 4-6-0 No. 61249 *FitzHerbert Wright* works a down express at Wickham Market Junction.

Plate 193: In this scene, Class B17/6, 3 cylinder 4-6-0 No. 61622 *Alnwick Castle* works a down express at Wickham Market Junction.

Plate 194: An up Yarmouth slow train passes Wickham Market Junction hauled by Class L1, 2-6-4T No. 67709. The Framlingham branch is seen diverging on the left of the picture.

Plate 195: The down 'Easterling' express hauled by a Class B17/6, 3 cylinder 4-6-0 No. 61649 *Sheffield United*, passes Wickham Market Junction. The name board was usually carried on the bracket beneath the chimney.

Plate 196: In this scene, on a snowy morning near Wickham Market Junction, the up morning train, behind Class B1, 4-6-0 No. 61054 is piloted by Class B12/3, 4-6-0 No. 61561.

Plate 197: A down slow train at Wickham Market Junction is headed by Class B17/6, 3 cylinder 4-6-0 No. 61631 *Serlby Hall*.

Plate 198: The sun creates a second image as Class B17/1, 3 cylinder 4-6-0 No. 61629 *Naworth Castle* hauls an up train at Wickham Market Junction.

Plate 199: With the Framlingham branch coming in on the right, Class B1, 4-6-0 No. 61160 passes Wickham Market Junction with a down express.

Plate 200: A Class B17/6, 3 cylinder 4-6-0 No. 61659 *East Anglian* loses steam as it heads an up express composed of Southern Region rolling stock. No. 61659 was streamlined in 1937 for working the 'East Anglian Express' but had its valances removed in 1942. It was rebuilt to its normal state in 1951.

Plate 201: This photograph shows the second of the streamlined 'Sandringham' Class, 3 cylinder 4-6-0s, No. 61670 *City of London*, which was treated in the same way as No. 61659. Both 61659 and 61670 worked consistently well from Yarmouth South Town over the East Suffolk line from 1951 until their withdrawal. Both locomotives retained the two lubricators on the right hand side in front of the leading splasher with which they had been fitted when streamlined in 1937. This photograph should be compared with Plate 66 which shows this locomotive as it was running semi-streamlined in 1949.

Plate 202: Class B17/1, 3 cylinder 4-6-0 No. 61660 *Hull City* works the morning down stock train near Wickham Market Junction.

Plate 203: A 'Britannia' Class 4-6-2 No. 70041 *Sir John Moore* powers an up Yarmouth and Lowestoft express at Wickham Market Junction on Sunday, 1st November 1959. From Monday 2nd November, the line from Beccles to Yarmouth South Town was closed, except for sugar beet traffic to St. Olaves, and to Aldeby which survived a little longer. No. 70041 is passing one of the then new Brush diesel locomotives, No. D5541, which was on ballasting duties.

Plate 204: A Class J15, 0-6-0 No. 65454 loses steam as she comes off the Framlingham branch and crosses over to the up road. No. 65454 was a Stratford locomotive (30A), but it spent its last weeks before withdrawal at Ipswich.

Plate 205: The Framlingham branch train wends it way through the beautiful countryside with Class F6, 2-4-2T No. 67230 in charge. It has just come on to the branch at Wickham Market Junction with Ray Moore on the footplate.

Plate 206: One of the early weed killing trains carries out its duties on the Framlingham branch near Marlesford. It is hauled by Class J15, 0-6-0 No. 65467.

Plate 207:   A 'Super Claud' Class D16/2, 4-4-0 No. 62591 waits at Parham on the evening train to Framlingham.

Plate 208:   Speeding through a cutting with a Framlingham College 'start of term' special from Liverpool St., Class B12/3, 4-6-0 No. 61535 approaches Framlingham. These specials ran from 1954 to 1958, the regular passenger service having ceased in 1952. The last special ran in April 1958 when, on arrival at Framlingham with empty coaching stock, the locomotive, a J15 0-6-0 required over an hour for a blow up, thus missing the London connection.

Plate 209: Another 'Framlingham College Special' leaves Framlingham behind Class B12/3, 4-6-0 No. 61537 creating a powerful scene.

Plate 210: It was very rare for a steam locomotive to become a total failure as it could usually limp along until help could be obtained. However, this scene shows Class F6, 2-4-2T No. 67230 having completely failed whilst working the branch train between Parham and Framlingham. The fire had to be thrown out hurriedly and a relief locomotive requested from Ipswich. This was sister locomotive Class F6, 2-4-2T No. 67239 which proceeded to propel the stricken train into Framlingham, the passengers having already been collected by taxi. The picture shows the train approaching Framlingham and I was very fortunate to be at the right place at the right time. The photograph was taken from a patient's garden as I was leaving after an emergency call.

Plate 211: After the war, Sunday excursions to London were very popular from country stations in East Anglia. This picture shows Class B12/3, 4-6-0 No. 61561 having just arrived with the empty coaching stock from Ipswich and running round its train over rails dated 1877. The branch locomotive, Class J15, 0-6-0 No. 65467, is on the shed road. The water tank was that originally supplied by Garrett's of Leiston in 1859. The branch set of coaches can be seen in the siding up at the station in the background.

Plate 212: Class J15, 0-6-0 No. 65447 propels its coaches into Framlingham for a Sunday excursion. On this occasion, the branch locomotive was Class E4, 2-4-0 No. 62789 seen on the shed road.

Plate 213: A 'Britannia' Class 4-6-2, No. 70001 *Lord Hurcomb* is pictured at Wickham Market in June 1951. It was the first time I had seen one of this class on the East Suffolk line. It was on a Saturday afternoon and it seems probable that it was the first time the crew had driven a 'Britannia'. Only the head of a state monopoly could come between No. 70000 *Britannia* and No. 70002 *Geoffrey Chaucer* in order of precedence.

Plate 214: The locomotive shed at Ipswich closed to steam in November 1959, except for the Snape branch freight locomotives which survived until March 1960. It had been a wonderful October, and a printers' strike prevented the winter timetables from being printed. The summer service, therefore, continued into November. This atmospheric view shows Class B1, 4-6-0 No. 61317 leaving Wickham Market on the up Sunday morning train for the last time. The following day diesel power took over.

Plate 215: One of the last visits of a 'Claud Hamilton' 4-4-0 to the East Suffolk line is seen in this view. It was taken on a Good Friday morning and shows Class D16/3, 4-4-0 No. 62613 piloting Class B17/6, 3 cylinder 4-6-0 No. 61622 *Alnwick Castle* on the up morning train leaving Wickham Market. No. 62613 was shedded at Yarmouth Vauxhall (32E) and was normally employed between there and Norwich.

Plate 216: A Class B17/1, 3 cylinder 4-6-0 No. 61660 *Hull City* leaves Wickham Market on an up express. It is seen taking the down road, as permanent way work was in progress on the up line.

Plate 217:   On a cold snowy morning, Class B17/1, 3 cylinder 4-6-0 No. 61629 *Naworth Castle* leaves Wickham Market.

Plate 218:   The down Sunday Halesworth milk train, hauled by Class L1, 2-6-4T No. 67775, passes through open country-side near Wickham Market.

Plate 219 (above): No mention of steam locomotives in East Anglia would be complete without reference to the Wissington Railway. This line, built without parliamentary sanction, ran from Abbey, on the Stoke Ferry branch, to serve isolated fenland farms. Later it was taken over by the predecessors of the British Sugar Corporation to serve their factory at Wissington. The fenland section was closed in 1957. This picture shows Hudswell Clarke 0-6-0T *Wissington* on the only remaining stretch of the fenland line. It continued to work until 1970 and is now on show at Sheringham, having been presented to the North Norfolk Railway by the British Sugar Corporation.

Plate 220 (right top): After a total ban on steam working over any section of British Rail, permission was given in 1974 for ▷ the use of steam-hauled specials over a few specially selected routes. One of these routes was from Manningtree to March, for the use of the renovated 5 ft. 7 in. Maunsell ex-Southern Railway 4-6-0 No. 841 *Greene King*, at this time preserved at Chappel, on the Stour Valley line. *Greene King* ran to Stockton and back under her own steam in 1975 and then made two more trips on the main line in 1976 and 1977 respectively. Unfortunately, delays were caused on both occasions by the locomotive, and permission to run on the main line again was withdrawn. This powerful scene shows S R Maunsell 5 ft. 7 in. 4-6-0 No. 841 *Greene King* climbing Haughley bank on the first special in 1976.

Plate 221 (right bottom): In conclusion, mention must be made of the magnificent live steam museum created by Mr Alan ▷ Bloom at his nurseries at Bressingham, near Diss. Here, a variety of steam locomotives can be seen, heard, and travelled on in perfect surroundings. This photograph shows Mr Alan Bloom, as so many thousands of people know him, standing in front of *Gwynedd* a 1 ft. 11 in. gauge 0-4-0T, built in 1883 by Hunslet and used on the Penrhyn Slate Quarry lines before coming to Bressingham. It takes a great man to turn his dreams into reality. Fortunately, Alan Bloom is one of these men. Instead of sitting back and bemoaning the diesels, like so many of his contemporaries, he set about to make his nursery garden at Bressingham into the unique steam centre it is today. He started from scratch, as Bressingham is several miles from the nearest railway line at Diss. But such was his sense of timing, that six days after the 'Britannia' Class 4-6-2 No. 70013 *Oliver Cromwell* had worked the final BR steam special from Manchester to Carlisle, it was safely installed at Bressingham. Alan Bloom appreciates that a locomotive in steam is a thing of beauty and that the more beautiful the surroundings, the more it would appeal to the public at large. It is when one visits other railway preservation centres and then returns to Bressingham, that one fully realizes what Alan Bloom has done for East Anglia and what a debt it owes to him.

Plate 222: And finally, it is to Bressingham that Bill Last comes, whenever he can, to drive once again a steam locomotive and to give such tremendous pleasure to so many people. This picture shows him preparing the Beyer-Garratt 0-4-4-0 *William Francis*, late of Baddesley Collieries, Atherstone. His own private lamps are in position and the locomotive is being prepared to the same high standard that he maintained on all his locomotives at Cambridge. I should like to thank Bill for all his help in preparing this book, and to wish him, together with all his friends, a long and happy life with more years to come of driving steam locomotives.